MW01164993

The Khalil Gibran Collection

Volume III

The
Khalil Gibran
Collection

Volume III

Copyright © 2012 Bottom of the Hill Publishing

All rights reserved. No part of this book may be used or reproduced in any manner without written permission except for brief quotations for review purposes only.

This book was written in the prevailing style of that period. Language and spelling have been left original in an effort to give the full flavor of this classic work.

Printed in the United States of America and Australia.

Bottom of the Hill Publishing

Memphis, TN

www.BottomoftheHillPublishing.com

ISBN: 978-1-61203-995-4

Contents

LAZARUS AND HIS BELOVED

THE CAST

Lazarus
Mary, his sister
Martha, his sister
The mother of Lazarus
Philip, a disciple
A Madman

THE SCENE

The garden outside of the home of Lazarus and his mother and sisters in Bethany.

Late afternoon of Monday, the day after the resurrection of Jesus of Nazareth from the grave.

At curtain rise: Mary is at right gazing up towards the hills. Martha is seated at her loom near the house door, left. The Madman is seated around the corner of the house, and against its wall, down left.

THE PLAY

Mary: *(Turning to Martha)* You do not work. You have not worked much lately.

Martha: You are not thinking of my work. My idleness makes you think of what our Master said. Oh, beloved Master!

The Madman: The day shall come when there will be no weaver, and no one to wear the cloth. We shall all stand naked in the sun.

(There is a long silence. The women do not appear to have heard The Madman speaking. They never hear him.)

Mary: It is getting late.

Martha: Yes, yes, I know. It is getting late.

(The mother enters, coming out from the house door.)

Mother: Has he not returned yet?

Martha: No, mother, he has not returned yet.

(The three women look towards the hills.)

The Madman: He himself will never return. All that you may see is a breath struggling in a body.

Mary: It seems to me that he has not yet returned from the other world.

Mother: The death of our Master has afflicted him deeply, and during these last days he has hardly eaten a morsel, and I know at night that he does not sleep. Surely it must have been the death of our Friend.

Martha: No, mother. There is something else; something I do not understand.

Mary: Yes, yes. There is something else. I know it, too. I have known it all these days, yet I cannot explain it. His eyes are deeper. He gazes at me as though he were seeing someone else through me. He is tender but his tenderness is for someone not here. And he is silent, silent as if the seal of death is yet upon his lips.

(A silence falls over the three women.)

The Madman: Everyone looks through everyone else to see someone else.

Mother: *(Breaking the silence)* Would that he'd return. Of late he

has spent too many hours among those hills alone. He should
be here with us.

Mary: Mother, he has not been with us for a long time.

Martha: Why, he has always been with us, only those three days!

Mary: Three days? Three days! Yes, Martha, you are right. It was
only three days.

Mother: I wish my son would return from the hills.

Martha: He will come soon, mother. You must not worry.

Mary: *(in a strange voice)* Sometimes I feel that he will never come
back from the hills.

Mother: If he came back from the grave, the surely he will come
back from the hills. And oh, my daughters, to think that the One
who gave us back his life was slain but yesterday.

Mary: Oh the mystery of it, and the pain of it.

Mother: Oh, to think that they could be so cruel to the One who
gave my son back to my heart.

(A silence)

Martha: But Lazarus should not stay so long among the hills.

Mary: It is easy for one in a dream to lose his way among the olive
groves. And I know a place where Lazarus loved to sit and dream
and be still. Oh, mother, it is beside a little stream. If you do not
know the place you could not find it. He took me there once, and
we sat on two stones, like children. It was spring, and little flowers were growing beside us. We often spoke of that place during
the winter season. And each time that he spoke of that place a
strange light came into his eyes.

The Madman: Yes, that strange light, that shadow cast by the
other light.

Mary: And mother, you know that Lazarus has always been away
from us, though he was always with us.

Mother: You say so many things I cannot understand. *(Pause)* I
wish my son would come back from the hills. I wish he would
come back! *(Pause)* I must go in now. The lentils must not be
overcooked.

(The mother exits through the door)

Martha: I wish I could understand all that you say, Mary. When
you speak it is as though someone else is speaking.

Mary: *(Her voice a little strange)* I know, my sister, I know. Whenever we speak it is someone else who is speaking.

(There is a prolonged silence. Mary is faraway in her thoughts, and

Martha watches her half-curiously. Lazarus enters, coming from the hills, back left. He throws himself upon the grass under the almond trees near the house.)

Mary: *(Running toward him)* Oh Lazarus, you are tired and weary. You should not have walked so far.

Lazarus: *(Speaking absently)* Walking, walking and going nowhere; seeking and finding nothing. But it is better to be among the hills.

The Madman: Well, after all it is a cubit nearer to the other hills.

Martha: *(After brief silence)* But you are not well, and you leave us all day long, and we are much concerned. What you came back, Lazarus, you made us happy. But in leaving us alone here you turn our happiness into anxiety.

Lazarus: *(Turning his face toward the hills)* Did I leave you long this day? Strange that you should call a moment among the hills a separation. Did I truly stay more than a moment among the hills?

Martha: You have been gone all day.

Lazarus: To think, to think! A whole day among the hills! Who would believe it?

(A silence. The mother enters, coming out from the house door.)

Mother: Oh, my son, I am glad you have come back. It is late and the mist is gathering upon the hills. I feared for you my son.

The Madman: They are afraid of the mist. And the mist is their beginning and the mist is their end.

Lazarus: Yes, I have come back to you from the hills. The pity of it, the pity of it all.

Mother: What is it Lazarus? What is the pity of it all?

Lazarus: Nothing, mother. Nothing.

Mother: You speak strangely. I do not understand you, Lazarus. You have said little since your home-coming. But whatever you have said has been strange to me.

Martha: Yes, strange.

(There is a pause.)

Mother: And now the mist is gathering here. Let us go into the house. Come, my children.

(The mother, after kissing Lazarus with wistful tenderness, enters the house.)

Martha: Yes, there is a chill in the air. I must take my loom and my linen indoors.

Mary: *(sitting down beside Lazarus on the grass under the almond trees, and speaking to Martha)* It is true the April evenings are not good for either your loom or your linen. Would you want me to help you take your loom indoors?

Martha: No, no. I can do it alone. I have always done it alone.

(Martha carries her loom into the house, then she returns for the linen, taking that in also. A wind passes by, shaking the almond tree, and a drift of petals falls over Mary and Lazarus.)

Lazarus: Even spring would comfort us, and even the trees would weep for us. All there is on earth, if all there is on earth could know our downfall and our grief, would pity us and weep for us.

Mary: But spring is with us, and though veiled with the veil of sorrow, yet it is spring. Let us not speak of pity. Let us rather accept both our spring and our sorrow with gratitude. And let us wonder in sweet silence at Him who gave you life yet yielded His own life. Let us not speak of pity, Lazarus.

Lazarus: Pity, pity that I should be torn away from a thousand thousand years of heart's desire, a thousand thousand years of heart's hunger. Pity that after a thousand thousand springs I am turned to this winter.

Mary: What do you mean, my brother? Why do you speak of a thousand thousand springs? You were but three days away from us. Three short days. But our sorrow was indeed longer than three days.

Lazarus: Three days? Three centuries, three aeons! All of time! All of time with the one my soul loved before time began.

The Madman: Yes, three days, three centuries, three aeons. Strange they would always weigh and measure. It is always a sundial and a pair of scales.

Mary: *(In amazement)* The one you soul loved before time began? Lazarus, why do you say these things? It is but a dream you dreamed in another garden. Now we are here in this garden, a stone's throw from Jerusalem. We are here. And you know well, my brother, that our Master would have you be with us in this awakening to dream of life and love; and He would have you an ardent disciple, a living witness of His glory.

Lazarus: There is no dream here and there is no awakening. You and I and this garden are but an illusion, a shadow of the real. The awakening is there where I was with my beloved and the reality.

Mary: *(Rising)* Your beloved?

Lazarus: *(Also rising)* My beloved.

The Madman: Yes, yes. His beloved, the space virgin, the beloved of everyman.

Mary: But where is your beloved? Who is your beloved?

Lazarus: My twin heart whom I sought here and did not find. Then death, the angel with winged feet, came and led my longing to her longing, and I lived with her in the very heart of God. And I became nearer to her and she to me, and we were one. We were a sphere that shines in the sun; and we were a song among the stars. All this, Mary, all this and more, till a voice, a voice from the depths, the voice of a world called me; and that which was inseparable was torn asunder. And the thousand thousand years with my beloved in space could not guard me from the power of that voice which called me back.

Mary: *(Looking unto the sky)* O blessed angels of our silent hours, make me to understand this thing! I would not be an alien in this new land discovered by death. Say more, my brother, go on. I believe in my heart I can follow you.

The Madman: Follow him, if you can, little woman. Shall the turtle follow the stag?

Lazarus: I was a stream and I sought the sea where my beloved dwells, and when I reached the sea I was brought to the hills to run again among the rocks. I was a song imprisoned in silence, longing for the heart of my beloved, and when the winds of heaven released me and uttered me in that green forest I was recaptured by a voice, and I was turned again into silence. I was a root in the dark earth, and I became a flower and then a fragrance in space rising to enfold my beloved, and I was caught and gathered by hand, and I was made a root again, a root in the dark earth.

The Madman: If you are a root you can always escape the tempests in the branches. And it is good to be a running stream even after you have reached the sea. Of course it is good for water to run upward.

Mary: *(To herself)* Oh strange, passing strange! *(To Lazarus)* But my brother it is good to be a running stream, and it is not good to be a song not yet sung, and it is good to be a root in the dark earth. The Master knew all this and He called you back to us that we may know there is no veil between life and death. Do you not see how one word uttered in love may bring together elements scattered by an illusion called death? Believe and have faith, for only in faith, which is our deeper knowledge, can you find comfort.

Lazarus: Comfort! Comfort the treacherous, the deadly! Comfort that cheats our senses and makes us slaves to the passing hour! I would not have comfort. I would have passion! I would burn in the cool space with my beloved. I would be in the boundless space with my mate, my other self. O Mary, Mary, you were once my sister, and we knew one another even when our nearest kin knew us not. Now listen to me, listen to me with your heart.

Mary: I am listening, Lazarus.

The Madman: Let the whole world listen. The sky will now speak to the earth, but the earth is deaf as you and I.

Lazarus: We were in space, my beloved and I, and we were all space. We were in light and we were all light. And we roamed even like the ancient spirit that moved upon the face of the waters; and it was forever the first day. We were love itself that dwells in the heart of the white silence. Then a voice like thunder, a voice like countless spears piercing the ether, cried out saying, "Lazarus, come forth!" And the voice echoed and re-echoed in space, and I, even as a flood tide became an ebbing tide; a house divided, a garment rent, a youth unspent, a tower that fell down, and out of its broken stones a landmark was made. A voice cried "Lazarus, come forth!" and I descended from the mansion of the sky to a tomb within a tomb, this body in a sealed cave.

The Madman: Master of the caravan, where are your camels and where are your men? Was it the hungry earth that swallowed them? Was it the simoom that shrouded them with sand? No! Jesus of Nazareth raised His hand, Jesus of Nazareth uttered a word; and tell me now, where are your camels and where are your men, and where are your treasures? In the trackless sand, in the trackless sand. But the moon will always come again.

Mary: Oh, it is like a dream dreamt upon a mountaintop. I know, my brother, I know the world you have visited, though I have never seen it. Yet all that you say is passing strange. It is a tale told by someone across a valley, and I can hardly hear it.

Lazarus: It is all so different across the valley. There is no weight there and there is no measure. You are with your beloved.

(A silence)

Lazarus: O my beloved! O my beloved fragrance in space! Wings that were spread for me! Tell me, tell me in the stillness of my heart, do you seek me, and was it pain to you to be separated from me? Was I also a fragrance and wings spread in space? And tell me now, my beloved, was there a double cruelty, was there a brother of His in another world who called you from life to death, and had you a mother and sisters and friends who deemed it a miracle? Was there a double cruelty performed in blessedness?

Mary: No, no, my brother. There is only one Jesus of one world. All else is but a dream, even as your beloved.

Lazarus: *(With great passion)* No, no! If He is not a dream then He is nothing. If He had not known what is beyond Jerusalem, then He is nothing. If He did not know my beloved in space then He was not the Master. O my friend Jesus, you once gave me a cup of wine across the table, and you said, "Drink this in remembrance of me." And you dipped a morsel of bread in the oil, and you said, "Eat this, it is my share of the loaf." O my friend, you have put your arm on my shoulder and called me "son." My mother and my sisters have said in their hearts, "He loves our Lazarus." And I loved you. And then you went away to build more towers in the sky, and I went to my beloved. Tell me now, tell me, why did you bring me back? Did you not know in your knowing heart that I was with my beloved? Did you not meet her in you wandering above the summits of Lebanon? Surely you saw her image in my eyes when I came and stood before you at the door of the tomb. And have you not a beloved in the sun? And would you have a greater one than yourself separate you from her? And after separation what would you say? What shall I say to you now?

The Madman: He bade me also to come back but I did not obey, and now they call me mad.

Mary: Lazarus, Have I a beloved in the sky? Has my longing created a being beyond this world? And must I die to be with him? Oh, my brother, tell me, have I a mate also? If this thing be so, how good it is to live and die, and live and die again; if a beloved awaits me, to fulfill all that I am, and I to fulfill all that he is!

The Madman: Everywoman has a beloved in the sky. The heart of everywoman creates a being in space.

Mary: *(Repeating softly as if to herself)* Have I a beloved in the sky?

Lazarus: I do not know. But if you had a beloved, an other self, somewhere, somewhen, and you should meet him, surely there would not be one to separate you from him.

The Madman: He may be here, and He may call her. But like many others she may not hear.

Lazarus: *(Coming to the center of stage)* To wait, to wait for each season to overcome another season; and then to wait for that season to be overcome by another; to watch all things ending before your own end comes-your end which is your beginning. To listen to all voices, and to know that they melt to silence, all save the voice of your heart that would cry even in sleep.

The Madman: The children of God married the children of men. Then they were divorced. Now, the children of men long for the children of God. I pity them all, the children of men and the children of God.

(A silence)

Martha: *(Appearing in the doorway)* Why don't you come into the house, Lazarus? Our mother has prepared the supper. *(With a little impatience)* Whenever you and Mary are together you talk and talk, and no one knows what you say.

(Martha stands for a sew seconds, then goes into the house.)

Lazarus: *(Speaking to himself, and as though he has not heard Martha)* Oh, I am spent. I am wasted, I am hungry and I am thirsty. Would that you could give me some bread and some wine.

Mary: *(Going to him and putting her arm around him)* I will, I will, my brother. But some into the house. Our mother has prepared the evening meal.

The Madman: He asks for bread which they cannot bake, and wine for which they have no bottles.

Lazarus: Did I say I was hungry and thirsty? I am not hungry for your bread, nor thirsty for your wine. I tell you I shall not enter a house until my beloved's hand is upon the latch of the door. I shall not sit at the feast till she be at my side.

(Mother peers from the house door.)

Mother: Now, Lazarus, why do you stay out in the mist? And you, Mary, why do you not come into the house? I have lit the candles and the food is upon the board, and yet you will stay out babbling and chewing your words in the dark.

Lazarus: Mine own mother would have me enter a tomb. She would have me eat and drink and she would even bid me sit among shrouded faces and receive eternity from withered hands and draw life from clay cups.

The Madman: White bird that flew southward where the sun loves all things, what held you in mid-air, and who brought you back? It was your friend, Jesus of Nazareth. He brought you back out of pity for the wingless who would not be along. Oh, white bird, it is cold here, and you shiver and the North wind laughs in your feathers.

Lazarus: You would be in a house and under a roof. You would be within four walls, with a door and a window. You would be here, and you are without vision. Your mind is here, and my spirit is there. All of you is upon the earth; all of me is in space. You creep into houses, and I flew beyond upon the mountaintop. You are all slaves, the one to the other, and you worship but yourselves. You sleep and you dream not; you wake but you walk not among the hills. And yesterday I was weary of you and of lives, and I sought the other world which you call death, and if I had died it was out of longing. Now, I stand here at this moment, rebelling against that which you call life.

Martha: (Who has come out of the house while Lazarus was speaking) But the Master saw our sorrow and our pain, and He called you back to us, and yet you rebel. Oh, what cloth, rebelling against its own weaver! What a house rebelling against its own builder!

Mary: He knew our hearts and He was gracious unto us, and when He met our mother and saw in her eyes a dead son, buried, then her sorrow held Him, and for a moment He was still, and He was silent. (Pause) Then we followed Him to your tomb.

Lazarus: Yes, it was my mother's sorrow, and your sorrow. It was pity, self-pity, that brought me back. How selfish is self-pity, and how deep. I say that I rebel. I say that divinity itself should not turn spring to winter. I had climbed the hills in longing, and your sorrow brought me back to this valley. You wanted a son and a brother to be with you through life. Your neighbours wanted a miracle. You and your neighbours, like your fathers and your forefathers, would have a miracle, that you may believe in the simplest things in life. How cruel you are and how hard are your hearts, and how dark is the night of your eyes. For that you bring down the prophets from their glory to you joys, and then you kill the prophets.

Martha: (with reproof) You call our sorrow self-pity. What is your wailing but self-pity? Be quiet, and accept the life the Master has given you.

Lazarus: He did not give me life, He gave you my life. He took my life from my own beloved, and gave it to you, a miracle to open your eyes and your ears. He sacrificed me even as He sacrificed Himself. (Speaking unto the sky) Father, forgive them. They know not what they do.

Mary: *(In awe)* It was He who said those very words, hanging upon the cross.

Lazarus: Yes, He said these words for me as for Himself, and for all the unknown who understand and are not understood. Did He not say these words when your tears begged Him for my life? It was your desire and not His will that bade His spirit to stand at the sealed door and urge eternity to yield me unto you. It was the ancient longing for a son and a brother that brought me back.

Mother: *(Approaches him and puts her arm around his shoulders)* Lazarus, you were ever an obedient son and a loving son. What has happened to you? Be with us, and forget all that troubles you.

Lazarus: *(Raising his hand)* My mother and my brothers and my sisters are those who hear my words.

Mary: These are also His words.

Lazarus: Yes, and He said these words for me as well as for Himself, and for all those who have earth for mother, and sky for father, and for all those who are born free of a people and a country and a race.

The Madman: Captain of my ship, the wind filled your sails, and you dared the sea; and you sought the blessed isles. What other wind changed your course, and why did you return to these shores? It was Jesus of Nazareth who commanded the wind with a breath of His own breath, and then filled the sail where it was empty, and emptied it where it was full.

Lazarus: *(Suddenly he forgets them all, and he raises his head, and opens his arms.)* O my beloved! There was dawn in your eyes, and in that dawn there was the silent mystery of a deep night, and the silent promise of a full day, and I was fulfilled, and I was whole. O my beloved, this life, this veil, is between us now. Must I live this death and die again that I may live again? Must needs linger until all these green things turn yellow and then naked again, and yet again? *(Pause)* Oh, I cannot curse Him. But why, of all men, why should I return? Why should I of all shepherds be driven back into the desert after the green pasture?

The Madman: If you were one of those who would curse, you would not have died so young.

Lazarus: Jesus of Nazareth, tell me now, why did you do this to me? Was it fair that I should be laid down, a humble lowly sorrowful stone leading to the height of your glory? Any one of the dead might have served to glorify you. Why have you separated this lover from his beloved? Why did you call me to a world which you knew in your heart you would leave? *(Then crying with a great voice)* Why – why – why did you call me from the living heart of eternity to this living death? O Jesus of Nazareth – I cannot curse you! I cannot curse you. I would bless you. *(Silence. Lazarus becomes as one whose strength has gone out in a stream. His head falls forward almost upon his breast. After a moment of awful silence, he raises his head again, and with a transfigured face he cries in a deep and thrilling voice.)* Jesus of Narareth! My friend! We have both been crucified. Forgive me! Forgive me. I bless you-now, and forevermore.

(At this moment the disciple appears running from the direction of the hills.)

Mary: Philip!

Philip: He is risen! The Master is risen from the dead and now He is gone to Galilee.

The Madman: He is risen, but He will be crucified again a thousand times.

Mary: Philip, my friend, what do you say?

Martha: *(Rushes toward the disciple, and grasps him by the arms)* How glad I am to see you again. But who has risen? Of whom are you speaking?

Mother: *(Walking toward him)* Come in, my son. You shall have supper with us tonight.

Philip: *(Unmoved by any of their words)* I say the Master has risen from the dead and has gone into Galilee.

(A deep silence falls.)

Lazarus: Now you shall all listen to me. If He has risen from the dead they will crucify Him again, but they shall not crucify Him alone. Now I shall proclaim Him, and they shall crucify me also.

(He turns in exaltation and walk in the direction of the hills.)

Lazarus: My mother and my sisters, I shall follow Him who gave me life until He gives me death. Yes, I too would be crucified, and that crucifixion will end this crucifixion.

(A silence)

Lazarus: Now I shall seek His spirit, and I shall be released. And though they bind me in iron chains I shall not be bound. And though a thousand mothers and a thousand thousand sisters shall hold my garments I shall not be held. I shall go with the

East wind where the East wind goes. And I shall seek my beloved in the sunset where all our days find peace. And I shall seek my beloved in the night where all the mornings sleep. And I shall be the one man among all men who twice suffered life, and twice death, and twice knew eternity.

(Lazarus looks into the face of his mother, then into the faces of his sisters, the at Philip's face; then again at his mother's face. Then as if he were a sleepwalker he turns and runs toward the hills. He disappears. They are all dazed and shaken.)

Mother: My son, my son, come back to me!

Mary: My brother, where are you going? Oh come, my brother, come back to us.

Martha: *(As if to herself)* It is so dark I know that he will lose his way.

Mother: *(Almost screaming)* Lazarus, my son!

(A silence)

Philip: He has gone where we all shall go. And he shall not return.

Mother: *(Going to the very back of the stage, close to where he has disappeared)* Lazarus, Lazarus, my son! Come back to me! *(She shrieks.)*

(There is a silence. The running steps of Lazarus are lost in the distance.)

The Madman: Now he is gone, and he is beyond your reach. And now your sorrow must seek another. *(He pauses)* Poor, poor Lazarus, the first of the martyrs, and the greatest of them all.

The Earth Gods

A one act play

THE EARTH GODS

When the night of the twelfth aeon fell,
And silence, the high tide of night, swallowed the hills,
The three earth-born gods, the Master Titans of life,
Appeared upon the mountains.
Rivers ran about their feet;
The mist floated across their breasts,
And their heads rose in majesty above the world.
Then they spoke, and like distant thunder
Their voices rolled over the plains.

FIRST GOD

The wind blows eastward;
I would turn my face to the south,
For the wind crowds my nostrils with the odors of dead things.

SECOND GOD

It is the scent of burnt flesh, sweet and bountiful.
I would breathe it.
FIRST GOD
It is the odor of mortality parching upon its own faint flame.
Heavily does it hang upon the air,
And like foul breath of the pit
It offends my senses.
I would turn my face to the scentless north.

SECOND GOD

It is the inflamed fragrance of brooding life
This I would breathe now and forever.
Gods live upon sacrifice,
Their thirst quenched by blood,
Their hearts appeased with young souls,
Their sinews strengthened by the deathless sighs
Of those who dwell with death;

Their thrones are built upon the ashes of generations.

FIRST GOD

Weary is my spirit of all there is.
I would not move a hand to create a world
Nor to erase one.
I would not live could I but die,
For the weight of aeons is upon me,
And the ceaseless moan of the seas exhausts my sleep.
Could I but lose the primal aim
And vanish like a wasted sun;
Could I but strip my divinity of its purpose
And breathe my immortality into space,
And be no more;
Could I but be consumed and pass from time's memory
Into the emptiness of nowhere!

THIRD GOD

Listen my brothers, my ancient brothers.
A youth in yonder vale
Is singing his heart to the night.
His lyre is gold and ebony.
His voice is silver and gold.

SECOND GOD

I would not be so vain as to be no more.
I could not but choose the hardest way;
To follow the seasons and support the majesty of the years;
To sow the seed and to watch it thrust through the soil;
To call the flower from its hiding place
And give it strength to nestle its own life,
And then to pluck it when the storm laughs in the forest;
To raise man from secret darkness,
Yet keep his roots clinging to the earth;
To give him thirst for life, and make death his cupbearer;
To endow him with love that waxeth with pain,
And exalts with desire, and increases with longing,
And fadeth away with the first embrace;
To girdle his nights with dreams of higher days,
And infuse his days with visions of blissful nights,
And yet to confine his days and his nights
To their immutable resemblance;
To make his fancy like the eagle of the mountain,
And his thought as the tempests of the seas,

And yet to give him hands slow in decision,
And feet heavy with deliberation;
To give him gladness that he may sing before us,
And sorrow that he may call unto us,
And then to lay him low,
When the earth in her hunger cries for food;
To raise his soul high above the firmament
That he may foretaste our tomorrow,
And to keep his body groveling in the mire
That he may not forget his yesterday.
Thus shall we rule man unto the end of time,
Governing the breath that began with his mother's crying,
And ends with the lamentation of his children.

FIRST GOD

My heart thirsts, yet I would not drink the faint blood of a feeble race,
For the cup is tainted, and the vintage therein is bitter to my
mouth.
Like thee I have kneaded the clay and fashioned it to breathing
forms
That crept out of my dripping fingers unto the marshes and the hills.
Like thee I have kindled the dark depths of beginning life
And watched it crawl from caves to rocky heights.
Like thee I have summoned spring and laid the beauty thereof
For a lure that seizes youth and binds it to generate and multiply.
Like thee I have led man from shrine to shrine,
And turned his mute fear of things unseen
To tremulous faith in us, the unvisited and the unknown.
Like thee I have ridden the wild tempest over his head
That he might bow before us,
And shaken the earth beneath him until he cried unto us;
And like thee, led the savage ocean against his nestled isle,
Till he hath died calling upon us.
All this have I done, and more.
And all that I have done is empty and vain.
Vain is the waking and empty is the sleep,
And thrice empty and vain is the dream.

THIRD GOD

Brothers, my august brothers,
Down in the myrtle grove
A girl is dancing to the moon,
A thousand dew-stars are in her hair,
About her feet a thousand wings.

SECOND GOD

We have planted man, our vine, and tilled the soil
In the purple mist of the first dawn.
We watched the lean branches grow,
And through the days of seasonless years
We nursed the infant leaves.
From the angry element we shielded the bud,
And against all dark spirits we guarded the flower.
And now that our vine hath yielded the grape
You will not take it to the winepress and fill the cup.
Whose mightier hand than yours shall reap the fruit?
And what nobler end than your thirst awaits the wine?
Man is food for the gods,
And the glory of man begins
When his aimless breath is sucked by gods' hallowed lips.
All that is human counts for naught if human it remain;
The innocence of childhood, and the sweet ecstasy of youth,
The passion of stern manhood, and the wisdom of old age;
The splendour of kings and the triumph of warriors,
The fame of poets and the honor of dreamers and saints;
All these and all that lieth therein is bred for gods.
And naught but bread ungraced shall it be
If the gods raise it not to their mouths.
And as the mute grain turns to love songs when swallowed by
the nightingale,
Even so as bread of gods shall man taste godhead.

FIRST GOD

Aye, man is meat for gods!
And all that is man shall come upon the gods' eternal board!
The pain of child-bearing and the agony of childbirth,
The blind cry of the infant that pierces the naked night,
And the anguish of the mother wrestling with the sleep she
craves,
To pour life exhausted from her breast;
The flaming breath of youth tormented,
And the burdened sobs of passion unspent;
The dripping brows of manhood tilling the barren land,
And the regret of pale old age when life against life's will
Calls to the grave.
Behold this is man!
A creature bred on hunger and made food for hungry gods.
A vine that creeps in dust beneath the feet of deathless death.

The flower that blooms in nights of evil shadows;
The grape of mournful days, and days of terror and shame.
And yet you would have me eat and drink.
You would bid me sit amongst shrouded faces
And draw my life from stony lips
And from withered hands receive my eternity.

THIRD GOD

Brothers, my dreaded brothers,
Thrice deep the youth is singing,
And thrice higher is his song.
His voice shakes the forest
And pierces the sky,
And scatters the slumbering of earth.

SECOND GOD

(Always unhearing)
The bee hums harshly in your ears,
And foul is the honey to your lips.
Fain would I comfort you,
But how shall I?
Only the abyss listens when gods call unto gods,
For measureless is the gulf that lies between divinities,
And windless is the space.
Yet I would comfort you,
I would make serene your clouded sphere;
And though equal we are in power and judgment,
I would counsel you.

When out of chaos came the earth, and we, sons of the beginning, beheld each other in the lustless light, we breathed the first hushed, tremulous sound that quickened the currents of air and sea.

Then we walked, hand in hand, upon the gray infant world, and out of the echoes of our first drowsy steps time was born, a fourth divinity, that sets his feet upon our footprints, shadowing our thoughts and desires, and seeing only with our eyes.

And unto earth came life, and unto life came the spirit, the winged melody of the universe. And we ruled life and spirit, and none save us knew the measure of the years nor the weight of years' nebulous dreams, till we, at noontide of the seventh aeon, gave the sea in marriage to the sun.

And from the inner chamber of their nuptial ecstasy, we brought man, a creature who, though yielding and infirm, bears ever the marks of his parentage.

Through man who walks earth with eyes upon the stars, we find pathways to earth's distant regions; and of man, the humble reed growing beside dark waters, we make a flute through whose hollowed heart we pour our voice to the silence-bound world. From the sunless north to the sun-smitten sand of the south.

From the lotus land where days are born
To perilous isles where days are slain,
Man the faint hearted, overbold by our purpose,
Ventures with lyre and sword.
Ours is the will he heralds,
And ours the sovereignty he proclaims,
And his love trodden courses are rivers, to the sea of our desires.
We, upon the heights, in man's sleep dream our dreams.
We urge his days to part from the valley of twilights
And seek their fullness upon the hills.
Our hands direct the tempests that sweep the world
And summon man from sterile peace to fertile strife,
And on to triumph.
In our eyes is the vision that turns man's soul to flame,
And leads him to exalted loneliness and rebellious prophecy,
And on to crucifixion.
Man is born to bondage,
And in bondage is his honor and his reward.
In man we seek a mouthpiece,
And in his life our self-fulfillment.

Whose heart shall echo our voice if the human heart is deafened with dust?

Who shall behold our shining if man's eye is blinded with night?

And what would you do with man, child of our earliest heart, our own self image?

THIRD GOD

Brothers, my mighty brothers,
The dancer's feet are drunk with songs.
They set the air a-throbbing,
And like doves her hands fly upward.

FIRST GOD

The lark calls to the lark,
But upward the eagle soars,
Nor tarries to hear the song.
You would teach me self love fulfilled in man's worship,

And content with man's servitude.
But myself love is limitless and without measure.
I would rise beyond my earthbound mortality
And throne me upon the heavens.
My arms would girdle space and encompass the spheres.
I would take the starry way for a bow,
And the comets for arrows,
And with the infinite would I conquer the infinite.
But you would not do this, were it in your power.
Forever as man is to man,
So are gods to gods.
Nay, you would bring to my weary heart
Remembrance of cycles spent in mist,
When my soul sought itself among the mountains
And mine eyes pursued their own image in slumbering waters;
Though my yesterday died in child-birth
And only silence visits her womb,
And the wind strewn sand nestles at her breast.
Oh yesterday, dead yesterday,
Mother of my chained divinity,
What super-god caught you in your flight
And made you breed in the cage?
What giant sun warmed your bosom
To give me birth?
I bless you not, yet I would not curse you;
For even as you have burdened me with life
So I have burdened man
But less cruel have I been.
I, immortal, made man a passing shadow;
And you, dying, conceived me deathless.
Yesterday, dead yesterday,
Shall you return with distant tomorrow,
That I may bring you to judgment?
And will you wake with life's second dawn
That I may erase your earth-clinging memory from the earth?
Would that you might rise with all the dead of yore,
Till the land choke with its own bitter fruit,
And all the seas be stagnant with the slain,
And woe upon woe exhaust earth's vain fertility.

THIRD GOD

Brother, my sacred brothers,
The girl has heard the song.
And now she seeks the singer.

Like a fawn in glad surprise
She leaps over rocks and streams
And turns her to every side.
Oh, the joy in mortal intent,
The eye of purpose half-born;
The smile on lips that quiver
With foretaste of promised delight!
What flower has fallen from heaven,
What flame has risen from hell.
That startled the heart of silence
To this breathless joy and fear?
What dream dreamt we upon the height,
What thought gave we to the wind
That woke the drowsing valley
And made watchful the night?

SECOND GOD

The sacred loom is given you,
And the art to weave the fabric.
The loom and the art shall be yours for evermore,
And yours the dark thread and the light,
And yours the purple and the gold.
Yet you would grudge yourself a raiment.
Your hands have spun man's soul
From living air and fire,
Yet now you would break the thread,
And lend your versed fingers to an idle eternity.

FIRST GOD

Nay, unto eternity unmoulded I would give my hands,
And to untrodden fields assign my feet.
What joy is there in songs oft heard,
Whose tune the remembering ear arrests
Ere the breath yields it to the wind?
My heart longs for what my heart conceives not,
And unto the unknown where memory dwells not
I would command my spirit.
Oh, tempt me not with glory possessed,
And seek not to comfort me with your dream or mine,
For all that I am, and all that there is on earth,
And all that shall be, inviteth not my soul.
Oh my soul,
Silent is thy face,
And in thine eyes the shadows of night are sleeping.

But terrible is thy silence,
And thou art terrible.

THIRD GOD

Brothers, my solemn brothers,
The girl has found the singer.
She sees his raptured face.
Panther-like she slips with subtle steps
Through rustling vine and fern.
And now amid his ardent cries
He gazes full on her.
Oh my brothers, my heedless brothers,
Is it some other god in passion
Who has woven this web of scarlet and white?
What unbridled star has gone astray?
Whose secret keepeth night from morning?
And whose hand is upon our world?

FIRST GOD

Oh my soul, my soul,
Thou burning sphere that girdles me,
How shall I guide thy course.
And unto what space direct thy eagerness?
Oh my mateless soul,
In thy hunger thou preyest upon thyself,
And with thine own tears thou wouldst quench thy thirst;
For night gathers not her dew into thy cup,
And the day brings thee no fruit.
Oh my soul, my soul,
Thou grounded ship laden with desire,
Whence shall come the wind to fill thy sail,
And what higher tide shall release thy rudder?
Weighed is thine anchor and thy wings would spread,
But the skies are silent above thee,
And the still sea mocks at thy immobility.
And what hope is there for thee and me?
What shifting of worlds, what new purpose in the heavens,
That shall claim thee?
Does the womb of the virgin infinite
Bear the seed of thy Redeemer,
One mightier than thy vision
Whose hand shall deliver thee from thy captivity?

SECOND GOD

Hold your importunate cry,
And the breath of your burning heart,
For deaf is the ear of the infinite,
And heedless is the sky.
We are the beyond and we are the Most High,
And between us and boundless eternity
Is naught save our unshaped passion
And the motive thereof.
You invoke the unknown,
And the unknown clad with moving mist
Dwells in your own soul.
Yea, in your own soul your Redeemer lies asleep,
And in sleep sees what your waking eye does not see.
And that is the secret of our being.
Would you leave the harvest ungathered,
In haste to sow again the dreaming furrow?
And wherefore spread you your cloud in trackless fields and desolate,
When your own flock is seeking you,
And would fain gather in your own shadow?
Forbear and look down upon the world.
Behold the unweaned children of your love.
The earth is your abode, and the earth is your throne;
And high beyond man's furtherest hope
Your hand upholds his destiny.
You would not abandon him
Who strives to reach you through gladness and through pain.
You would not turn away your face from the need in his eyes.

FIRST GOD

Does dawn hold the heart of night unto her heart?
Or shall the sea heed the bodies of her dead?
Like dawn my soul rises within me
Naked and unencumbered.
And like the unresting sea
My heart casts out a perishing wrack of man and earth.
I would not cling to that clings to me.
But unto that that rises beyond my reach I would arise.

THIRD GOD

Brothers, behold, my brothers,
They meet, two star-bound spirits in the sky encountering.
In silence they gaze the one upon the other.
He sings no more,
And yet his sunburnt throat throbs with the song;

And in her limbs the happy dance is stayed
But not asleep.
Brothers, my strange brothers,
The night waxeth deep,
And brighter is the moon,
And twixt the meadow and the sea
A voice in rapture calleth you and me.

SECOND GOD

To be, to rise, to burn before the burning sun,
To live, and to watch the nights of the living
As Orion watches us!
To face the four winds with a head crowned and high,
And to heal the ills of man with our tideless breath!
The tentmaker sits darkly at his loom,
And the potter turns his wheel unaware;
But we, the sleepless and the knowing,
We are released from guessing and from chance.
We pause not nor do we wait for thought.
We are beyond all restless questioning.
Be content and let the dreaming go.
Like rivers let us flow to ocean
Unwounded by the edges of the rocks;
And when we reach her heart and are merged,
No more shall we wrangle and reason of tomorrow.

FIRST GOD

Oh, this ache of ceaseless divining,
This vigil of guiding the day unto twilight,
And the night unto dawn;
This tide of ever remembering and forgetting;
This ever sowing destinies and reaping but hopes;
This changeless lifting of self from dust to mist,
Only to long for dust, and to fall down with longing unto dust,
And still with greater longing to seek the mist again.
And this timeless measuring of time.
Must my soul needs to be a sea whose currents forever confound
one another,
Or the sky where the warring winds turn hurricane?
Were I man, a blind fragment,
I could have met it with patience.
Or if I were the Supreme Godhead,
Who fills the emptiness of man and of gods,
I would be fulfilled.

But you and I are neither human,
Nor the Supreme above us.
We are but twilights ever rising and ever fading
Between horizon and horizon.
We are but gods holding a world and held by it,
Fates that sound the trumpets
Whilst the breath and the music come from beyond.
And I rebel.
I would exhaust myself to emptiness.
I would dissolve myself afar from your vision,
And from the memory of this silent youth, our younger brother,
Who sits beside us gazing into yonder valley,
And though his lips move, utters not a word.

THIRD GOD

I speak, my unheeding brothers,
I do indeed speak,
But you hear only your own words.
I bid you see your glory and mine,
But you turn, and close your eyes,
And rock your thrones.
Ye sovereigns who would govern the above world and the world
beneath,
God self-bent, whose yesterday is ever jealous of your tomorrow,
Self-weary, who would unleash your temper with speech
And lash our orb with thunderings!
Your feud is but the sounding of an Ancient Lyre
Whose strings have been half forgotten by His fingers
Who has Orion for a harp and the Pleiades for cymbals.
Even now, while you are muttering and rumbling,
His harp rings, His cymbals clash,
And I beseech you hear his song.
Behold, man and woman,
Flame to flame,
In white ecstasy.
Roots that suck at the breast of purple earth,
Flame flowers at the breasts of the sky.
And we are the purple breast,
And we are the enduring sky.
Our soul, even the soul of life, your soul and mine,
Dwells this night in a throat enflamed,
And garments the body of a girl with beating waves.
Your scepter cannot sway this destiny,
Your weariness is but ambition.

This and all is wiped away
In the passion of a man and a maid.

SECOND GOD

Yea, what of this love of man and woman?
See how the east wind dances with her dancing feet,
And the west wind rises singing with his song.
Behold our sacred purpose now enthroned,
In the yielding of a spirit that sings to a body that dances.

FIRST GOD

I will not turn my eyes downward to the conceit of earth,
Nor to her children in their slow agony that you call love.
And what is love,
But the muffled drum and leads the long procession of sweet
uncertainty
To another slow agony?
I will not look downward.
What is there to behold
Save a man and a woman in the forest that grew to trap them
That they might renounce self
And parent creatures for our unborn tomorrow?

THIRD GOD

Oh, the affliction of knowing,
The starless veil of prying and questioning
Which we have laid upon the world;
And the challenge to human forbearance!
We would lay under a stone a waxen shape
And say, It is a thing of clay,
And in clay let it find its end.
We would hold in our hands a white flame
And say in our heart,
It is a fragment of ourselves returning,
A breath of our breath that had escaped,
And now haunts our hands and lips for more fragrance.
Earth gods, my brothers,
High upon the mountain,
We are still earth-bound,
Through man desiring the golden hours of man's destiny.
Shall our wisdom ravish beauty from his eyes?
Shall our measures subdue his passion to stillness,
Or to our own passion?
What would your armies of reasoning

Where love encamps his host?
They who are conquered by love,
And upon whose bodies love's chariot ran
From sea to mountain
And again form mountain to the sea,
Stand even now in a shy half-embrace.
Petal unto petal they breathe the sacred perfume,
Soul to soul they find the soul of life,
And upon their eyelids lies a prayer
Unto you and unto me.
Love is a night bent down to a bower anointed,
A sky turned meadow, and all the stars to fireflies.
True it is, we are the beyond,
And we are the most high.
But love is beyond our questioning,
And love outsoars our song.

SECOND GOD

Seek you a distant orb,
And would not consider this star
Where your sinews are planted?
There is no center in space
Save where self is wedded to self,
And beauty filling our hands to shame our lips.
The most distant is the most near.
And where beauty is, there are all things.
Oh, lofty dreaming brother,
Return to us from time's dim borderland!
Unlace your feet from no-where and no-when,
And dwell with us in this security
Which your hand intertwined with ours
Has built stone upon stone.
Cast off your mantle of brooding,
And comrade us, masters of the young earth green and warm.

FIRST GOD

Eternal Altar! Wouldst thou indeed this night
A god for sacrifice?
Now then, I come, and coming I offer up
My passion and my pain.
Lo, there is the dancer, carved out of our ancient eagerness,
And the singer is crying mine own songs unto the wind.
And in that dancing and in that singing
A god is slain within me.

My god-heart within my human ribs
Shouts to my god-heart in mid-air.
The human pit that wearied me calls to divinity.
The beauty that we have sought from the beginning
Calls unto divinity.
I heed, and I have measured the call,
And now I yield.
Beauty is a path that leads to self self-slain.
Beat your strings
I will to walk the path.
It stretches ever to another dawn.

THIRD GOD

Love triumphs.
The white and green of love beside a lake,
And the proud majesty of love in tower or balcony;
Love in a garden or in the desert untrodden,
Love is our lord and master.
It is not a wanton decay of the flesh,
Nor the crumbling of desire
When desire and self are wrestling;
Nor is it flesh that takes arms against the spirit.
Love rebels not.
It only leaves the trodden way of ancient destinies for the sacred grove,
To sing and dance its secret to eternity.
Love is youth with chains broken,
Manhood made free from the sod,
And womanhood warmed by the flame
And shining with the light of heaven deeper than our heaven.
Love is a distant laughter in the spirit.
It is a wild assault that hushes you to your awakening.
It is a new dawn unto the earth,
A day not yet achieved in your eyes or mine,
But already achieved in its own greater heart.
Brothers, my brothers,
The bride comes from the heart of dawn,
And the bridegroom from the sunset.
There is a wedding in the valley.
A day too vast for recording.

SECOND GOD

Thus has it been since the first morn
Discharged the plains to hill and vale,
And thus shall it be to the last even-tide.

Our roots have brought forth the dancing branches in the valley,
And we are the flowering of the song-scent that rises to the
heights.
Immortal and mortal, twin rivers calling to the sea.
There is no emptiness between call and call,
But only in the ear.
Time maketh our listening more certain,
And giveth it more desire.
Only doubt in mortal hushes the sound.
We have outsoared the doubt.
Man is a child of our younger heart.
Man is god in slow arising;
And betwixt his joy and his pain
Lies our sleeping, and the dreaming thereof.

FIRST GOD

Let the singer cry, and let the dancer whirl her feet
And let me be content awhile.
Let my soul be serene this night.
Perchance I may drowse, and drowsing
Behold a brighter world
And creatures more starry supple to my mind.

THIRD GOD

Now I will rise and strip me of time and space,
And I will dance in that field untrodden,
And the dancer's feet will move with my feet;
And I will sing in that higher air,
And a human voice will throb within my voice.
We shall pass into the twilight;
Perchance to wake to the dawn of another world.
But love shall stay,
And his finger-marks shall not be erased.
The blessed forge burns,
The sparks rise, and each spark is a sun.
Better it is for us, and wiser,
To seek a shadowed nook and sleep in our earth divinity,
And let love, human and frail, command the coming day.

Short Works

Chapter 1

The New Frontier

There are in the Middle East today two challenging ideas: old and new. The old ideas will vanish because they are weak and exhausted. There is in the Middle East an awakening that defies slumber. This awakening will conquer because the sun is its leader and the dawn is its army.

In the fields of the Middle East, which have been a large burial ground, stand the youth of Spring calling the occupants of the sepulchers to rise and march toward the new frontiers. When the Spring sings its hymns the dead of the winter rise, shed their shrouds and march forward.

There is on the horizon of the Middle East a new awakening; it is growing and expanding; it is reaching and engulfing all sensitive, intelligent souls; it is penetrating and gaining all the sympathy of noble hearts.

The Middle East, today, has two masters. One is deciding, ordering, being obeyed; but he is at the point of death. But the other one is silent in his conformity to law and order, calmly awaiting justice; he is a powerful giant who knows his own strength, confident in his existence and a believer in his destiny.

There are today, in the Middle East, two men: one of the past and one of the future. Which one are you? Come close, let me look at you and let me be assured by your appearance and your conduct if you are one of those coming into the light or going into the darkness.

Come and tell me who and what are you.

Are you a politician asking what your country can do for you or a zealous one asking what you can do for your country? If you are the first, then you are a parasite; is the second, then you are an oasis in a desert.

Are you a merchant utilizing the need of society for the necessities of life, for monopoly and exorbitant profit? Or a sincere, hardworking and diligent man facilitating the exchange between the weaver and the farmer? Are you charging a reasonable profit as a middleman between supply and demand? If you are the first, then you are a criminal whether you live in a palace or a prison. If you are the second, then you are a charitable man whether you are thanked or denounced by people.

Are you a religious leader, weaving for your body a gown out of the ignorance of the people, fashioning a crown out of the simplicity of their hearts and pretending to hate the devil merely to live upon his income? Or are you a devout and a pious man who sees in the piety of the individual the foundation for a progressive nation, and who can see through a profound search in the depth of his own soul a ladder to the eternal soul that directs the world? If you are the first, then you are a heretic, a disbeliever in God even if you fast by day and pray by night. If you are the second, then you are a violet in the garden of truth even though its fragrance is lost upon the nostrils of humanity or whether its aroma rises into that rare air where the fragrance of flowers is preserved.

Are you a newspaperman who sells his idea and principle in the slave market, who lives on the misery of people like a buzzard which descends only upon a decaying carcass? Or are you a teacher on the platform of the city gathering experience from life and presenting it to the people as sermons you have learned? If you are the first, then you are a sore and an ulcer. If you are the second, then you are a balsam and a medicine.

Are you a governor who denigrates himself before those who appoint him and denigrates those whom he is to govern, who never raises a hand unless it is to reach into pockets and who does not take a step unless it is for greed? Or are you a faithful servant who serves only the welfare of the people? If you are the first, then you are as a tare in the threshing floor of the nations; and if the second, then you are a blessing upon its granaries.

Are you a husband who allows for himself what he disallows for his wife, living in abandonment with the key of her prison in his boots, gorging himself with his favorite food while she sits, by herself, before an empty dish? Or are you a companion, taking no action except hand in hand, nor doing anything unless she gives her thoughts and opinions, and sharing with her your happiness and success? If you are the first, then you are a remnant of a tribe which, still dressing in the skins of animals, vanished long before leaving the caves; and if you are the second, then you are a leader in a nation moving in the dawn toward the light of justice and wisdom.

Are you a searching writer full of self-admiration, keeping his head in the valley of a dusty past, where the ages discarded the remnant of its clothes and useless ideas? Or are you a clear thinker examining what is good and useful for society and spending your life in building what is useful and destroying what is harmful? If you are the first, then you are feeble and stupid, and if you are the second, then you are bread for the hungry and water for the thirsty.

Are you a poet, who plays the tambourine at the doors of emirs, or the one who throws the flowers during weddings and who walks in processions with a sponge full of warm water in his mouth, a sponge to be pressed by his tongue and lips as soon as he reaches the cemetery? Or have you a gift which God has placed in your hands on which to play heavenly melodies which draw our hearts toward the beautiful in life? If you are the first, then you are a juggler who evokes in our soul that which is contrary to what you intend. If you are the second, then you are love in our hearts and a vision in our minds.

In the Middle East there are two processions: One procession is of old people walking with bent backs, supported with bent canes; they are out of breath though their path is downhill.

The other is a procession of young men, running as if on winged feet, and jubilant as with musical strings in their throats, surmounting obstacles as if there were magnets drawing them up on the mountainside and magic enchanting their hearts.

Which are you and in which procession do you move?

Ask yourself and meditate in the still of the night; find if you are a slave of yesterday or free for the morrow.

I tell you that the children of yesteryears are walking in the funeral of the era that they created for themselves. They are pulling a rotted rope that might break soon and cause them to drop into a forgotten abyss. I say that they are living in homes with weak foundations; as the storm blows -- and it is about to blow -- their homes will fall upon their heads and thus become their tombs. I say that all their thoughts, their sayings, their quarrels, their compositions, their books and all their work are nothing but chains dragging them because they are too weak to pull the load.

But the children of tomorrow are the ones called by life, and the follow it with steady steps and heads high, they are the dawn of new frontiers, no smoke will veil their eyes and no jingle of chains will drown out their voices. They are few in number, but the difference is as between a grain of wheat and a stack of hay. No one knows them but they know each other. They are like the summits, which can see or hear each other -- not like caves, which cannot hear or see. They are the seed dropped by the hand of God in the field, breaking through its pod and waving its sapling leaves before the face of the sun. It shall grow into a mighty tree, its root in the heart of the earth and its branches high in the sky.

Chapter 2
I Believe in You

I believe in you, and I believe in your destiny.

I believe that you are contributors to this new civilization.

I believe that you have inherited from your forefathers an ancient dream, a song, a prophecy, which you can proudly lay as a gift of gratitude upon the lap of America.

I believe that you can say to the founders of this great nation, "Here I am, a youth, a young tree whose roots were plucked from the hills of Lebanon, yet I am deeply rooted here, and I would be fruitful."

And I believe that you can say to Abraham Lincoln, the blessed, "Jesus of Nazareth touched your lips when you spoke, and guided your hand when you wrote; and I shall uphold all that you have said and all that you have written."

I believe that you can say to Emerson and Whitman and James, "In my veins runs the blood of the poets and wise men of old, and it is my desire to come to you and receive, but I shall not come with empty hands."

I believe that even as your fathers came to this land to produce riches, you were born here to produce riches by intelligence, by labor.

I believe that it is in you to be good citizens.

And what is it to be a good citizen?

It is to acknowledge the other person's rights before asserting your own, but always to be conscious of your own.

It is to be free in word and deed, but it is also to know that your freedom is subject to the other person's freedom.

It is to create the useful and the beautiful with your own hands, and to admire what others have created in love and with faith.

It is to produce by labor and only by labor, and to spend less than you have produced that your children may not be dependent upon the state for support when you are no more.

It is to stand before the towers of New York and Washington, Chicago and San Francisco saying in your heart, "I am the descendant of a people that built Damascus and Byblos, and Tyre and Sidon and Antioch, and now I am here to build with you, and with a will."

You should be proud of being an American, but you should also be proud that your fathers and mothers came from a land upon which God laid His gracious hand and raised His messengers.

Young Americans of Syrian origin, I believe in you.

Chapter 3

My Countrymen

What do you seek, my countrymen?
Do you desire that I build for
You gorgeous palaces, decorated
With words of empty meaning, or
Temples roofed with dreams? Or
Do you command me to destroy what
The liars and tyrants have built?
Shall I uproot with my fingers
What the hypocrites and the wicked
Have implanted? Speak your insane
Wish!

What is it you would have me do,
My countrymen? Shall I purr like
The kitten to satisfy you, or roar
Like the lion to please myself? I
Have sung for you, but you did not
Dance; I have wept before you, but
You did not cry. Shall I sing and
Weep at the same time?

Your souls are suffering the pangs
Of hunger, and yet the fruit of
Knowledge is more plentiful than
The stones of the valleys.
Your hearts are withering from
Thirst, and yet the springs of
Life are streaming about your
Homes -- why do you not drink?

The sea has its ebb and flow,
The moon has its fullness and
Crescents, and the ages have
Their winter and summer, and all
Things vary like the shadow of
An unborn god moving between
Earth and sun, but truth cannot
Be changed, nor will it pass away;
Why, then, do you endeavour to

Disfigure its countenance?

I have called you in the silence
Of the night to point out the
Glory of the moon and the dignity
Of the stars, but you startled
From your slumber and clutched
Your swords in fear, crying,
"Where is the enemy? We must kill
Him first!" At morningtide, when
The enemy came, I called to you
Again, but now you did not wake
From your slumber, for you were
Locked in fear, wrestling with
The processions of specters in
Your dreams.

And I said unto you, "Let us climb
To the mountain top and view the
Beauty of the world." And you
Answered me, saying, "In the depths
Of this valley our fathers lived,
And in its shadows they died, and in
Its caves they were buried. How can
We depart this place for one which
They failed to honour?"

And I said unto you, "Let us go to
The plain that gives its bounty to
The sea." And you spoke timidly to
Me, saying, "The uproar of the abyss
Will frighten our spirits, and the
Terror of the depths will deaden
Our bodies."

I have loved you, my countrymen, but
My love for you is painful to me
And useless to you; and today I
Hate you, and hatred is a flood
That sweeps away the dry branches
And quavering houses.

I have pitied your weakness, my
Countrymen, but my pity has but
Increased your feebleness, exalting
And nourishing slothfulness which
Is vain to life. And today I see

Your infirmity which my soul loathes
And fears.

I have cried over your humiliation
And submission, and my tears streamed
Like crystalline, but could not sear
Away your stagnant weakness; yet they
Removed the veil from my eyes.
My tears have never reached your
Petrified hearts, but they cleansed
The darkness from my inner self.

Today I am mocking at your suffering,
For laughter is a raging thunder that
Precedes the tempest and never comes
After it.

What do you desire, my countrymen?
Do you wish for me to show you
The ghost of your countenance on
The face of still water? Come,
Now, and see how ugly you are!

Look and meditate! Fear has
Turned your hair grey as the
Ashes, and dissipation has grown
Over your eyes and made them into
Obscured hollows, and cowardice
Has touched your cheeks that now
Appear as dismal pits in the
Valley, and death has kissed
Your lips and left them yellow
As the autumn leaves.

What is it that you seek, my
Countrymen? What ask you from
Life, who does not any longer
Count you among her children?
Your souls are freezing in the
Clutches of the priests and
Sorcerers, and your bodies
Tremble between the paws of the
Despots and the shedders of
Blood, and your country quakes
Under the marching feet of the
Conquering enemy; what may you
Expect even though you stand

Proudly before the face of the
Sun? Your swords are sheathed
With rust, and your spears are
Broken, and your shields are
Laden with gaps, why, then, do
You stand in the field of battle?

Hypocrisy is your religion, and
Falsehood is your life, and
Nothingness is your ending; why,
Then, are you living? Is not
Death the sole comfort of the
Miserable?

Life is a resolution that
Accompanies youth, and a diligence
That follows maturity, and a
Wisdom that pursues senility; but
You, my countrymen, were born old
And weak. And your skins withered
And your heads shrank, whereupon
You become as children, running
Into the mire and casting stones
Upon each other.

Knowledge is a light, enriching
The warmth of life, and all may
Partake who seek it out; but you,
My countrymen, seek out darkness
And flee the light, awaiting the
Coming of water from the rock,
And your nation's misery is your
Crime. I do not forgive you
Your sins, for you know what you
Are doing.

Humanity is a brilliant river
Singing its way and carrying with
It the mountains' secrets into
The heart of the sea; but you,
My countrymen, are stagnant
Marshes infested with insects
And vipers.

The spirit is a sacred blue
Torch, burning and devouring
The dry plants, and growing

With the storm and illuminating
The faces of the goddesses; but
You, my countrymen, your souls
Are like ashes which the winds
Scatter upon the snow, and which
The tempests disperse forever in
The valleys.

Fear not the phantom of death,
My countrymen, for his greatness
And mercy will refuse to approach
Your smallness; and dread not the
Dagger, for it will decline to be
Lodged in your shallow hearts.

I hate you, my countrymen, because
You hate glory and greatness. I
Despise you because you despise
Yourselves. I am your enemy, for
You refuse to realize that you are
The enemies of the goddesses.

Chapter 4

Satan

The people looked upon Father Samaan as their guide in the field of spiritual and theological matters, for he was an authority and a source of deep information on venial and mortal sins, well versed in the secrets of paradise, hell, and purgatory.

Father Samaan's mission in North Lebanon was to travel from one village to another, preaching and curing the people from the spiritual disease of sin, and saving them from the horrible trap of Satan. The Reverend Father waged constant war with Satan. The fellahin honoured and respected this clergyman, and were always anxious to buy his advice or prayers with pieces of gold and silver; and at every harvest they would present him with the finest fruits of their fields.

One evening in autumn, as Father Samaan walked his way towards a solitary village, crossing those valleys and hills, he heard a painful cry emerging from a ditch at the side of the road. He stopped and looked in the direction of the voice, and saw an unclothed man lying on the ground. Streams of blood oozed from deep wounds in his head and chest. He was moaning painfully for aid, saying, "Save me, help me. Have mercy on me, I am dying." Father Samaan looked with perplexity at the sufferer, and said within himself, "This man must be a thief. He probably tried to rob the wayfarers and failed. Someone has wounded him, and I fear that should he die I may be accused of having taken his life."

Having thus pondered the situation, he resumed his journey, whereupon the dying man stopped him, calling out, "Do not leave me! I am dying!" Then the Father meditated again, and his face became pale as he realized he was refusing to help. His lips quivered, but he spoke to himself, saying, "He must surely be one of the madmen wandering in the wilderness. The sight of his wounds brings fear into my heart; what shall I do? Surely a spiritual doctor is not capable of treating flesh-wounded bodies." Father Samaan walked ahead a few paces when the near-corpse uttered a painful plaint that melted the heart of the rock and he gasped, "Come close to me! Come, for we have been friends a long time. You are Father Samaan, the good shepherd, and I am not a thief nor a madman. Come close, and do not let me die in this deserted place. Come, and I will tell you who I am."

Father Samaan came close to the man, knelt, and stared at him;
but he saw a strange face with contrasting features; he saw intelligence with slyness, ugliness with beauty, and wickedness with
softness. He withdrew to his feet sharply, and exclaimed, "Who are
you?"

With a fainting voice, the dying man said, "Fear me not, Father,
for we have been strong friends for long. Help me to stand, and
take me to the nearby streamlet and cleanse my wounds with your
linens." And the Father inquired, "Tell me who you are, for I do not
know you, nor even remember having seen you."

And the man replied with an agonizing voice, "You know my
identity! You have seen me one thousand times and you speak of
me each day. I am dearer to you than your own life." And the Father reprimanded, "You are a lying imposter! A dying man should
tell the truth. I have never seen your evil face in my entire life. Tell
me who you are, or I will suffer you to die, soaked in your escaping life." And the wounded man moved slowly and looked into the
clergyman's eyes, and upon his lips appeared a mystic smile; and
in a quiet, deep and smooth voice he said, "I am Satan."

Upon hearing the fearful word, Father Samaan uttered a terrible
cry that shook the far corners of the valley; then he stared, and
realized that the dying man's body, with its grotesque distortions,
coincided with the likeness of Satan in a religious picture hanging
on the wall of the village church. He trembled and cried out, saying, "God has shown me your hellish image and justly caused me
to hate you; cursed be you for evermore! The mangled lamb must
be destroyed by the shepherd lest he will infect the other lambs!"

Satan answered, "Be not in haste, Father, and lose not this fleet-
ing time in empty talk. Come and close my wounds quickly, before
life departs from my body." And the clergyman retorted, "The hands
which offer a daily sacrifice to God shall not touch a body made of
the secretion of hell. You must die accursed by the tongues of the
ages, and the lips of humanity, for you are the enemy of humanity,
and it is your avowed purpose to destroy all virtue."

Satan moved in anguish, raising himself upon one elbow, and
responded, "You know not what you are saying, nor understand
the crime you are committing upon yourself. Give heed, for I will
relate my story. Today I walked alone in this solitary valley. When
I reached this place, a group of angels descended to attack, and
struck me severely; had it not been for one of them, who carried a
blazing sword with two sharp edges, I would have driven them off,
but I had no power against the brilliant sword." And Satan ceased
talking for a moment, as he pressed a shaking hand upon a deep

wound in his side. Then he continued, "The armed angel -- I be-lieve he was Michael -- was an expert gladiator. Had I not thrown myself to the friendly ground and feigned to have been slain, he would have torn me into brutal death."

With voice of triumph, and casting his eyes heavenwards, the Father offered, "Blessed be Michael's name, who has saved hu-manity from this vicious enemy."

And Satan protested, "My disdain for humanity is not greater than your hatred for yourself. You are blessing Michael, who never has come to your rescue. You are cursing me in the hour of my defeat, even though I was, and still am, the source of your tran-quility and happiness. You deny me your blessing, and extend not your kindness, but you live and prosper in the shadow of my being. You have adopted my existence as an excuse and weapon for your career, and you employ my name in justification for your deeds. Has not my past caused you to be in need of my present and future? Have you reached your goal in amassing the required wealth? Have you found it impossible to extract more gold and sil-ver from your followers, using my kingdom as a threat?

"Do you not realize that you will starve to death if I were to die? What would you do tomorrow if you allowed me to die today? What vocation would you pursue if my name disappeared? For decades you have been roaming these villages and warning the people against falling into my hands. They have bought your advice with their poor dinars and with the products of their land. What would they buy from you tomorrow, if they discovered that their wicked enemy no longer existed? Your occupation would die with me, for the people would be safe from sin. As a clergyman, do you not realize that Satan's existence alone has created his enemy, the Church? That ancient conflict is the secret hand which removes the gold and silver from the faithful's pocket and deposits it forev-er into the pouch of the preacher and the missionary. How can you permit me to die here, when you know it will surely cause you to lose your prestige, your church, your home, and your livelihood?"

Satan became silent for a moment and his humility was now converted into a confident independence, and he continued, "Fa-ther, you are proud, but ignorant. I will disclose to you the history of belief, and in it you will find he truth which joins both of our beings, and ties my existence with your very conscience.

"In the first hour of the beginning of time, man stood before the face of the sun and stretched forth his arms and cried for the first time, saying, 'Behind the sky there is a great and loving and be-nevolent God.' The man turned his back to the great circle of light and saw his shadow upon the earth, and he hailed, 'In the depths of the earth there is a dark evil who loves wickedness.'

"And the man walked towards his cave, whispering to himself, "I am between two compelling forces, one in whom I must take refuge, and the other against whom I must struggle.' And the ages marched in procession while man existed between two powers, one that he blessed because it exalted him, and one that he cursed because it frightened him. But he never perceived the meaning of a blessing or of a curse; he was between the two, like a tree between summer, when it blooms, and winter, when it shivers.

"When a man saw the dawn of civilization, which is human understanding, the family as a unit came into being. Then came the tribes, whereupon labour was divided according to ability and inclination; one clan cultivated the land, another built shelters, others wove raiment or hunted food. Subsequently divination made its appearance upon the earth, and this was the first career adopted by man which possessed no essential urge or necessity."

Satan ceased talking for a moment. Then he laughed and his mirth shook the empty valley, but his laughter reminded him of his wounds, and he placed his hand on his side, suffering with pain. He steadied himself and continued, "Divination appeared and grew on earth in strange fashion.

"There was a man in the first tribe called La Wiss. I know not the origin of his name. He was an intelligent creature, but extremely indolent and he detested work in the cultivation of land, construction of shelters, grazing of cattle, or any pursuit requiring bodily movement or exertion. And since food, during that era, could not be obtained except by arduous toil, La Wiss slept many nights with an empty stomach.

"One summer night, as the members of that clan were gathered round the hut of their chief, talking of the outcome of their day and waiting for their slumber time, a man suddenly leaped to his feet, pointed towards the moon, and cried out, saying, 'Look at the night god! His face is dark, and his beauty has vanished, and he has turned into a black stone hanging in the dome of the sky!' The multitude gazed at the moon, shouted in awe, and shook with fear, as if the hands of darkness had clutched their hearts, for they saw the night god slowly turning into a dark ball which changed the bright countenance of the earth and caused the hills and valleys before their eyes to disappear behind a black veil.

"At that moment, La Wiss, who had seen an eclipse before, and understood its simple cause, stepped forward to make much of this opportunity. He stood in the midst of the throng, lifted his hands to the sky, and in a strong voice he addressed them, saying, 'Kneel and pray, for the evil god of obscurity is locked in struggle with the illuminating night god; if the evil god conquers him, we will all perish, but if the night god triumphs over him, we will remain alive. Pray now and worship. Cover your faces with earth. Close your eyes, and lift not your heads towards the sky, for he who witnesses the two gods wrestling will lose his sight and mind, and will remain blind and insane all his life! Bend your heads low, and with all your hearts urge the night god against his enemy, who is our mortal enemy!'

"Thus did La Wiss continue talking, using many cryptic words of his own fabrication which they had never heard. After this crafty deception, as the moon returned to its previous glory, La Wiss raised his voice louder than before and said impressively, 'Rise now, and look at the night god who has triumphed over his evil enemy. He is resuming his journey among the stars. Let it be known that through your prayers you have helped him to overcome the devil of darkness. He is well pleased now, and brighter than ever.'

"The multitude rose and gazed at the moon that was shining in full beam. Their fear became tranquility, and their confusion was now joy. They commenced dancing and singing and striking with their thick sticks upon sheets of iron, filling the valleys with their clamour and shouting.

"That night, the chief of the tribe called La Wiss and spoke to him, saying, 'You have done something that no man has ever done. You have demonstrated knowledge of a hidden secret that no other among us understands. Reflecting the will of my people, you are to be the highest ranking member, after me, in the tribe. I am the strongest man, and you are the wisest and most learned person. You are the medium between our people and the gods, whose desires and deeds you are to interpret, and you will teach us those things necessary to gain their blessings and love.'

"And La Wiss slyly assured, 'Everything the human god reveals to me in my divine dreams will be conveyed to you in awakeness, and you may be confident that I will act directly between you and him.' The chief was assured, and gave La Wiss two horses, seven calves, seventy sheep and seventy lambs; and he spoke to him, saying, 'The men of the tribe shall build for you a strong house, and we will give you at the end of each harvest season a part of the crop of the land so you may live as an honourable and respected master.'

"La Wiss rose and started to leave, but the chief stopped him, saying, 'Who and what is the one whom you call the human god?

Who is this daring god who wrestles with the glorious night god? We have never pondered him before.' La Wiss rubbed his forehead and answered him, saying, 'My honourable master, in the olden time, before the creation of man, all the gods were living peacefully together in an upper world behind the vastness of the stars. The god of gods was their father, and knew what they did not know, and did what they were unable to do. He kept for himself the divine secrets that existed beyond the eternal laws. During the seventh epoch of the twelfth age, the spirit of Bahtaar, who hated the great god, revolted and stood before his father, and said, 'Why do you keep for yourself the power of great authority upon all creatures, hiding away from us the secrets and laws of the universe? Are we not your children who believe in you and share with you the great understanding and the perpetual being?'

"The god of gods became enraged and said, 'I shall preserve for myself the primary power and the great authority and the essential secrets, for I am the beginning and the end.'

"And Bahtaar answered him saying, 'Unless you share with me your might and power, I and my children and my children's children will revolt against you!' At that moment, the god of gods stood upon his throne in the deep heavens, and drew forth a sword, and grasped the sun as a shield; and with a voice that shook all corners of the eternity he shouted out, saying, 'Descend, you evil rebel, to the dismal lower world where darkness and misery exist! There you shall remain in exile, wandering until the sun turns into ashes and the stars into dispersed particles!' In that hour, Bahtaar descended from the upper world into the lower world, where all the evil spirits dwelt. Thereupon, he swore by the secret of life that he would fight his father and brothers by trapping every soul who loved them.'

"As the chief listened, his forehead wrinkled and his face turned pale. He ventured, 'Then the name of the evil god is Bahtaar?' and La Wiss responded, 'His name was Bahtaar when he was in the upper world, but when he entered into the lower world, he adopted successively the names Baalzaboul, Satanail, Balial, Zamiel, Ahriman, Mara, Abdon, Devil, and finally Satan, which is the most famous.'

"The chief repeated the word 'Satan' many times with a quivering voice that sounded like the rustling of the dry branches at the passing of the wind; then he asked, 'Why does Satan hate man as much as he hates the gods?'

"And La Wiss responded quickly, 'He hates man because man is a descendant of Satan's brothers and sisters.' The chief exclaimed,

'Then Satan is the cousin of man!' In a voice mingled with confusion and annoyance, he retorted, 'Yes, master, but he is their great enemy who fills their days with misery and their nights with horrible dreams. He is the power who directs the tempest towards their hovels, and brings famine upon their plantation, and disease upon them and their animals. He is an evil and powerful god; he is wicked, and he rejoices when we are in sorrow, and he mourns when we are joyous. We must, through my konwledge, examine him thoroughly, in order to avoid his evil; we must study his character, so we will not step upon his trap-laden path.'

"The chief leaned his head upon his thick stick and whispered, saying, 'I have learned now the inner secret of that strange power who directs the tempest towards our homes and brings the pestilence upon us and our cattle. The people shall learn all that I have comprehended now, and La Wiss will be blessed, honoured and glorified for revealing to them the mystery of their powerful enemy, and directing them away from the road of evil.'

"And La Wiss left the chief of the tribe and went to his retiring place, happy over his ingenuity, and intoxicated with the wine of his pleasure and fancy. For the first time, the chief and all the tribe, except La Wiss, spent the night slumbering in beds surrounded by horrible ghosts, fearful spectres, and disturbing dreams."

Satan ceased talking for a moment, while Father Samaan stared at him as one bewildered, and upon the Father's lips appeared the sickly laughter of death. Then Satan continued, "Thus divination came to this earth, and thus was my existence the cause for its appearance. La Wiss was the first who adopted my cruelty as a vocation. After the death of La Wiss, this occupation circulated through his children and prospered until it became a perfect and divine profession, pursued by those whose minds are ripe with knowledge, and whose souls are noble, and whose hearts are pure, and whose fancy is vast.

"In Babylon, the people bowed seven times in worshipping before a priest who fought me with his chantings. In Nineveh, they looked upon a man, who claimed to have known my inner secrets, as a golden link between God and man. In Tibet, they called the person who wrestled with me the son of the sun and moon. In Byblus, Ephesus and Antioch, they offered their children's lives in sacrifice to my opponents. In Jerusalem and Rome, they placed their lives in the hands of those who claimed they hated me and fought me with all their might.

"In every city under the sun my name was the axis of the educational circle of religion, arts, and philosophy. Had it not been for me, no temples would have been built, no towers or palaces would have been erected. I am the courage that creates resolution in man. I am the source that provokes originality of thought. I am the hand that moves man's hands. I am Satan everlasting. I am Satan whom people fight in order to keep themselves alive. If they cease struggling against me, slothfulness will deaden their minds and hearts and souls, in accordance with the weird penalties of their tremendous myth.

'I am the enraged and mute tempest who agitates the minds of man and the hearts of women. And in fear of me, they will travel to places of worship to condemn me, or to places of vice to make me happy by surrendering to my will. The monk who prays in the silence of the night to keep me away from his bed is like the prostitute who invites me to her chamber. I am Satan everlasting and eternal.

"I am the builder of convents and monasteries upon the foundation of fear. I build wine shops and wicked houses upon the foundations of lust and self-gratification. If I cease to exist, fear and enjoyment will be abolished from the world, and through their disappearance, desires and hopes will cease to exist in the human heart. Life will become empty and cold, like a harp with broken strings. I am Satan everlasting.

"I am the inspiration of falsehood, slander, treachery, deceit and mockery, and if these elements were to be removed from this world, human society would become like a deserted field in which naught would thrive but thorns of virtue. I am Satan everlasting.

"I am the father and mother of sin, and if sin were to vanish, the fighters of sin would vanish with it, along with their families and structures.

"I am the heart of all evil. Would you wish for human motion to stop through cessation of my heartbeat? Would you accept the result after destroying the cause? I am the cause! Would you allow me to die in this deserted wilderness? Do you desire to sever the bond that exists between you and me? Answer me, clergyman!"

And Satan stretched his arms and bent his head forward and gasped deeply; his face turned to grey and he resembled one of those Egyptian statues laid waste by the ages at the side of the Nile. Then he fixed his glittering eyes upon Father Samaan's face, and said, in a faltering voice, "I am tired and weak. I did wrong by using my waning strength to speak on things you already know. Now you may do as you please. You may carry me to your home and treat my wounds, or leave me in this place to die."

Father Samaan quivered and rubbed his hands nervously, and

with apology in his voice he said, "I know now what I had not known an hour ago. Forgive my ignorance. I know that your existence in this world creates temptation, and temptation is a measurement by which God adjudges the value of human souls. It is a scale which Almighty God uses to weigh the spirits. I am certain that if you die, temptation will die, and with its passing, death will destroy the ideal power which elevates and alerts man.

"You must live, for if you die and the people know it, their fear of hell will vanish and they will cease worshipping, for naught would be sin. You must live, for in your life is the salvation of humanity from vice and sin.

"As to myself, I shall sacrifice my hatred for you on the altar of my love for man."

Satan uttered a laugh that rocked the ground, and he said, "What an intelligent person you are, Father! And what wonderful knowledge you possess in theological facts! You have found, through the power of your knowledge, a purpose for my existence which I had never understood, and now we realize our need for each other.

"Come close to me, my brother; darkness is submerging the plains, and half of my blood has escaped upon the sand of this valley, and naught remains of me but the remnants of a broken body which death shall soon buy unless you render aid." Father Samaan rolled the sleeves of his robe and approached, and lifted Satan to his back and walked towards his home.

In the midst of those valleys, engulfed with silence and embellished with the veil of darkness, Father Samaan walked towards the village with his back bent under his heavy burden. His black raiment and long beard were spattered with blood streaming from above him, but he struggled forward, his lips moving in fervent prayer for the life of the dying Satan.

Chapter 5

You Have Your Lebanon and I Have My Lebanon

You have your Lebanon and its dilemma. I have my Lebanon and its beauty. Your Lebanon is an arena for men from the West and men from the East.

My Lebanon is a flock of birds fluttering in the early morning as shepherds lead their sheep into the meadow and rising in the evening as farmers return from their fields and vineyards.

You have your Lebanon and its people. I have my Lebanon and its people.

Yours are those whose souls were born in the hospitals of the West; they are as ship without rudder or sail upon a raging sea.... They are strong and eloquent among themselves but weak and dumb among Europeans.

They are brave, the liberators and the reformers, but only in their own area. But they are cowards, always led backwards by the Europeans. They are those who croak like frogs boasting that they have rid themselves of their ancient, tyrannical enemy, but the truth of the matter is that this tyrannical enemy still hides within their own souls. They are the slaves for whom time had exchanged rusty chains for shiny ones so that they thought themselves free. These are the children of your Lebanon. Is there anyone among them who represents the strength of the towering rocks of Lebanon, the purity of its water or the fragrance of its air? Who among them vouchsafes to say, "When I die I leave my country little better than when I was born"?

Who among them dare to say, "My life was a drop of blood in the veins of Lebanon, a tear in her eyes or a smile upon her lips"?

Those are the children of your Lebanon. They are, in your estimation, great; but insignificant in my estimation.

Let me tell you who are the children of my Lebanon.

They are farmers who would turn the fallow field into garden and grove.

They are the shepherds who lead their flocks through the valleys to be fattened for your table meat and your woolens.

They are the vine-pressers who press the grape to wine and boil it to syrup.

They are the parents who tend the nurseries, the mothers who spin the silken yarn.

They are the husbands who harvest the wheat and the wives who gather the sheaves.

They are the builders, the potters, the weavers and the bell-casters.

They are the poets who pour their souls in new cups.

They are those who migrate with nothing but courage in their hearts and strength in their arms but who return with wealth in their hands and a wreath of glory upon their heads.

They are the victorious wherever they go and loved and respected wherever they settle.

They are the ones born in huts but who died in palaces of learning.

These are the children of Lebanon; they are the lamps that cannot be snuffed by the wind and the salt which remains unspoiled through the ages.

They are the ones who are steadily moving toward perfection, beauty, and truth.

What will remain of your Lebanon after a century? Tell me! Except bragging, lying and stupidity? Do you expect the ages to keep in its memory the traces of deceit and cheating and hypocrisy? Do you think the atmosphere will preserve in its pockets the shadows of death and the stench of graves?

Do you believe life will accept a patched garment for a dress? Verily, I say to you that an olive plant in the hills of Lebanon will outlast all of your deeds and your works; that the wooden plow pulled by the oxen in the crannies of Lebanon is nobler than your dreams and aspirations.

I say to you, while the conscience of time listened to me, that the songs of a maiden collecting herbs in the valleys of Lebanon will outlast all the uttering of the most exalted prattler among you. I say to you that you are achieving nothing. If you knew that you are accomplishing nothing, I would feel sorry for you, but you know it not.

You have your Lebanon and I have my Lebanon.

Chapter 6

Your Thought and Mine

Your thought is a tree rooted deep in the soil of tradition and whose branches grow in the power of continuity. My thought is a cloud moving in the space. It turns into drops which, as they fall, form a brook that sings its way into the sea. Then it rises as vapour into the sky. Your thought is a fortress that neither gale nor the lightning can shake. My thought is a tender leaf that sways in every direction and finds pleasure in its swaying. Your thought is an ancient dogma that cannot change you nor can you change it. My thought is new, and it tests me and I test it morn and eve.

You have your thought and I have mine.

Your thought allows you to believe in the unequal contest of the strong against the weak, and in the tricking of the simple by the subtle ones. My thought creates in me the desire to till the earth with my hoe, and harvest the crops with my sickle, and build my home with stones and mortar, and weave my raiment with woolen and linen threads. Your thought urges you to marry wealth and notability. Mine commends self-reliance. Your thought advocates fame and show. Mine counsels me and implores me to cast aside notoriety and treat it like a grain of sand cast upon the shore of eternity. Your thought instills in your heart arrogance and superiority. Mine plants within me love for peace and the desire for independence. Your thought begets dreams of palaces with furniture of sandalwood studded with jewels, and beds made of twisted silk threads. My thought speaks softly in my ears, "Be clean in body and spirit even if you have nowhere to lay your head." Your thought makes you aspire to titles and offices. Mine exhorts me to humble service.

You have your thought and I have mine.

Your thought is social science, a religious and political dictionary. Mine is simple axiom. Your thought speaks of the beautiful woman, the ugly, the virtuous, the prostitute, the intelligent, and the stupid. Mine sees in every woman a mother, a sister, or a daughter of every man. The subjects of your thought are thieves, criminals, and assassins. Mine declares that thieves are the creatures of monopoly, criminals are the offspring of tyrants, and assassins are akin to the slain. Your thought describes laws, courts, judges, punishments. Mine explains that when man makes a law, he either violates it or obeys it. If there is a basic law, we are all one before it. He who disdains the mean is himself mean. He who vaunts his scorn of the sinful vaunts his disdain of all humanity. Your thought concerns the skilled, the artist, the intellectual, the philosopher, the priest. Mine speaks of the loving and the affectionate, the sincere, the honest, the forthright, the kindly, and the martyr. Your thought advocates Judaism, Brahmanism, Buddhism, Christianity, and Islam. In my thought there is only one universal religion, whose varied paths are but the fingers of the loving hand of the Supreme Being. In your thought there are the rich, the poor, and the beggared. My thought holds that there are no riches but life; that we are all beggars, and no benefactor exists save life herself.

You have your thought and I have mine.

According to your thought, the greatness of nations lies in their politics, their parties, their conferences, their alliances and treaties. But mine proclaims that the importance of nations lies in work – work in the field, work in the vineyards, work with the loom, work in the tannery, work in the quarry, work in the timberyard, work in the office and in the press. Your thought holds that the glory of the nations is in their heroes. It sings the praises of Rameses, Alexander, Caesar, Hannibal, and Napoleon. But mine claims that the real heroes are Confucius, Lao-Tse, Socrates, Plato, Abi Taleb, El Gazali, Jalal Ed-din-el Roumy, Copernicus, and Pasteur. Your thought sees power in armies, cannons, battleships, submarines, aeroplanes, and poison gas. But mine asserts that power lies in reason, resolution, and truth. No matter how long the tyrant endures, he will be the loser at the end. Your thought differentiates between pragmatist and idealist, between the part and the whole, between the mystic and materialist. Mine realizes that life is one and its weights, measures and tables do not coincide with your weights, measures and tables. He whom you suppose an idealist may be a practical man.

You have your thought and I have mine.

Your thought is interested in ruins and museums, mummies and petrified objects. But mine hovers in the ever-renewed haze and clouds. Your thought is enthroned on skulls. Since you take pride in it, you glorify it too. My thought wanders in the obscure and distant valleys. Your thought trumpets while you dance. Mine prefers the anguish of death to your music and dancing. Your thought is the thought of gossip and false pleasure. Mine is the thought of him who is lost in his own country, of the alien in his own nation, of the solitary among his kinfolk and friends.

You have your thought and I have mine.

Chapter 7

The Flute

Al-Nay (The Flute)

بعـــد أن يفـــنى الوجـــود
أعطـــنى النـــاى و غـــنى
وأنيـــن النـــاى يبقـــى
بعـــد أن يفـــنى الوجـــود

Give me the Nay and sing,
The secret song of eternity.
The laments of the Nay will linger
Beyond the decline of existence.

Chosen the forest dwelling
Rather than the castle?
Have you followed the stream
And climbed the rocks?
Have you anointed your body
With fragrance distilled in light?
Have you been drunk with dawn
In the goblets full of pure air?

Have you, like me,
Sat down at dusk,
Among the glowing languor
Of vines laden with grapes?
Have you lain down on the grass at night
And covered yourself with heavens,
Opening your heart to the future,
Forgetful of the past?

Give me the Nay and sing,
The song in tune with hearts.
The laments of the Nay will linger
Beyond the fading of sins.
Give me the Nay and sing,
Unmindful of troubles and cures.
For each man
Is nothing more than a watercolor sketch.

Chapter 8

History and the Nation

By the side of a rivulet that meandered among the rocks at the foot of Lebanon's Mountain sat a shepherdess surrounded by her flock of lean sheep grazing upon dry grass. She looked into the distant twilight as if the future were passing before her. Tears had jeweled her eyes like dew-drops adorning flowers. Sorrow had caused her lips to open that it might enter and occupy her sighing heart. After sunset, as the knolls and hills wrapped themselves in shadow, History stood before the maiden. He was an old man whose white hair fell like snow over his breast and shoulders, and in his right hand he held a sharp sickle. In a voice like the roaring sea he said, "Peace unto you, Syria."

The virgin rose, trembling with fear. "What do you wish of me, History?" she asked. Then she pointed to her sheep. "This is the remnant of a healthy flock that once filled this valley. This is all that your covetousness has left me. Have you come now to sate your greed on that?"

"These plains that were once so fertile have been trodden to barren dust by your trampling feet. My cattle that once grazed upon flowers and produced rich milk, now gnaw at thistles that leave them gaunt and dry.

"Fear God, oh History, and afflict me no more. The sight of you has made me detest life, and the cruelty of your sickle has caused me to love Death.

"Leave me in my solitude to drain the cup of sorrow—my best wine. Go, History, to the West where Life's wedding feast is being celebrated. Here let me lament the bereavement you have prepared for me."

Concealing his sickle under the folds of his garment, History looked upon her as a loving father looks upon his child, and said, "Oh Syria, what I have taken from you were my own gifts. Know that you sister-nations are entitled to a part of the glory which was yours. I must give to them what I gave you. Your plight is like that of Egypt, Persia and Greece, for each one of them also has a lean flock and dry pasture. Oh Syria, that which you call degradation is an indispensable sleep from which you will draw strength. The flower does not return to life save through death, and love does not grow except after separation."

The old man came close to the maiden, stretched forth his hand and said, "Shake my hand, oh Daughter of the Prophets." And she shook his hand and looked at him from behind a screen of tears and said, "Farewell, History, farewell." And he responded, "Until we meet again Syria, until we meet again."

And the old man disappeared like swift lightning, and the shepherdess called her sheep and started on her way, saying to herself, "Shall there be another meeting?"

Sand and Foam

I AM forever walking upon these shores,
Betwixt the sand and the foam.
The high tide will erase my foot-prints,
And the wind will blow away the foam.
But the sea and the shore will remain
Forever.

———————

Once I filled my hand with mist.
Then I opened it, and lo, the mist was a worm.
And I closed and opened my hand again, and behold there was a bird.
And again I closed and opened my hand, and in Its hollow stood a man with a sad face turned upward.
And again I closed my hand, and when I opened it there was naught but mist.
But I heard a song of exceeding sweetness.

———————

It was but yesterday I thought myself a fragment quivering without rhythm in the sphere of life.
Now I know that I am the sphere, and all life in rhythmic fragments moves within me.

———————

They say to me in their awakening, "You and the world you live in are but a grain of sand upon the infinite shore of an infinite sea."
And in my dream I say to them, "I am the infinite sea, and all worlds are but grains of sand upon my shore."

———————

Only once have I been made mute. It was when a man asked me, "Who are you?"

———————

The first thought of God was an angel.
The first word of God was a man.

———————

We were fluttering, wandering, longing creatures a thousand thousand years before the sea and the wind in the forest gave us words.

———————

Now how can we express the ancient of days in us with only the sounds of our yesterdays?

The Sphinx spoke only once, and the
Sphinx said, "A grain of sand is a desert, and a desert is a grain
of sand; and now let us be silent again."
I heard the Sphinx, but I did not understand.

Once I saw the face of a woman, and I beheld all her children not
yet born.
And a woman looked upon my face and she knew all my forefathers, dead before she was born.

Now would I fulfill myself. But how shall
I unless I become a planet with intelligent lives dwelling upon it?
Is not this every man's goal?

A pearl is a temple built by pain around a grain of sand.

What longing built our bodies and around what grains?

When God threw me, a pebble, into this wondrous lake 1 disturbed its surface with countless circles.
But when I reached the depths I became very still.

Give me silence and I will outdare the night.

I had a second birth when my soul and my body loved one another and were married.

Once I knew a man whose ears were exceedingly keen, but he
was dumb. He had lost his tongue in a battle.
I know now what battles that man fought before the great silence
came. I am glad he is dead.
The world Is not large enough for two of us.

Long did I lie in the dust of Egypt, silent and unaware of the
seasons.
Then the sun gave me birth, and I rose and walked upon the
banks of the Nile,
Singing with the days and dreaming with the nights.
And now the sun treads upon me with a thousand feet that I may
lie again in the dust of Egypt.
But behold a marvel and a riddle!
The very sun that gathered me cannot scatter me.

Still erect am I, and sure of foot do I walk upon the banks of the Nile.

Remembrance Is a form of meeting.

Forgetfulness Is a form of freedom.

We measure time according to the movement of countless suns; and they measure time by little machines in their little pockets.

Now tell me, how could we ever meet at the same place and the same time?

Space is not space between the earth and the sun to one who looks down from the windows of the Milky Way.

Humanity is a river of light running from ex-eternity to eternity.

Do not the spirits who dwell in the ether envy man his pain?

On my way to the Holy City I met another pilgrim and I asked him, "Is this indeed the way to the Holy City?"

And he said, "Follow me, and you will reach the Holy City in a day and a night."

And I followed him. And we walked many days and many nights, yet we did not reach the Holy City.

And what was to my surprise, he became angry with me because he had misled me.

Make me, O God, the prey of the lion, ere
You make the rabbit my prey.

One may not reach the dawn save by the path of the night.

My house says to me, "Do not leave me, for here dwells your past."

And the road says to me, "Come and follow me, for I am your future."

And I say to both my house and the road,

"I have no past, nor have I a future. If I stay here, there is a going in my staying; and if I go there Is a staying in my going. Only love and death change all things."

How can I lose faith in the justice of life, when the dreams of those who sleep upon feathers are not more beautiful than the dreams of those who sleep upon the earth?

Strange, the desire for certain pleasures is a part of my pain.

Seven times have I despised my soul:
The first time when I saw her being meek that she might attain height.
The second time when I saw her limping before the crippled.
The third time when she was given to choose between the hard and the easy, and she chose the easy.
The fourth time when she committed a wrong, and comforted herself that others also commit wrong.
The fifth time when she forbore for weakness, and attributed her patience to strength.
The sixth time when she despised the ugliness of a face, and knew not that it was one of her own masks.
And the seventh time when she sang a song of praise, and deemed It a virtue.

I am ignorant of absolute truth. But I am humble before my ignorance, and therein lies my honour and my reward.

There is a space between man's imagination and man's attainment that may only be traversed by his longing.

Paradise is there, behind that door, in the next room; but I have lost the key.
Perhaps I have only mislaid it.

You are blind and I am deaf and dumb, so let us touch hands and understand.

The significance of man is not in what he attains, but rather in what he longs to attain.

Some of us are like ink and some like paper.
And if it were not for the blackness of us, some of us would be dumb.
And if it were not for the whiteness of some of us, some of us would be blind.

Give me an ear and I will give you a voice.

Our mind is a sponge; our heart is a stream.

Is it not strange that most of us choose sucking rather than running?

———————

When you long for blessings that you may not name, and when you grieve knowing not the cause, then indeed you are growing with all things that grow, and rising toward your greater self.

———————

"When one Is drunk with a vision, he deems his faint expression of it the very wine.

———————

You drink wine that you may be intoxicated; and I drink that it may sober me from that other wine.

———————

When my cup is empty I resign myself to its emptiness; but when it is half full I resent its half-fullness.

———————

The reality of the other person is not in what he reveals to you, but in what he cannot reveal to you.

———————

Therefore, if you would understand him, listen not to what he says but rather to what he does not say.

———————

Half of what I say is meaningless; but I say it so that the other half may reach you.

———————

A sense of humour is a sense of proportion.

———————

My loneliness was born when men praised my talkative faults and blamed my silent virtues.

———————

When Life does not find a singer to sing her heart she produces a philosopher to speak her mind.

———————

A truth is to be known always, to be uttered sometimes.

———————

The real in us is silent; the acquired is talkative.

———————

The voice of life in me cannot reach the ear of life in you; but let us talk that we may not feel lonely.

———————

When two women talk they say nothing; when one woman speaks she reveals all of life.

———————

Frogs may bellow louder than bulls, but they cannot drag the plough in the field nor turn the wheel of the winepress, and of their skins you cannot make shoes.

————

Only the dumb envy the talkative.

————

If winter should say, "Spring is in my heart," who would believe winter?

————

Every seed Is a longing.

————

Should you really open your eyes and see, you would behold your image in all images.

And should you open your ears and listen, you would hear your voice in all voices.

————

It takes two of us to discover truth: one to utter it and one to understand it.

————

Though the wave of words is forever upon us, yet our depth is forever silent.

————

Many a doctrine is like a window pane. We see truth through it, but it divides us from truth.

————

Now let us play hide and seek. Should you hide in my heart it would not be difficult to find you. But should you hide behind your own shell, then it would be useless for anyone to seek you.

————

A woman may veil her face with a smile.

————

How noble is the sad heart who would sing a joyous song with joyous hearts.

————

He who would understand a woman, or dissect genius, or solve the mystery of silence is the very man who would wake from a beautiful dream to sit at a breakfast table.

————

I would walk with all those who walk. I would not stand still to watch the procession passing by.

————

You owe more than gold to him who serves you. Give him of your heart or serve him.

————

Nay, we have not lived in vain. Have they not built towers of our bones?

————————

Let us not be particular and sectional. The mind and the scorpion's tail rise in glory from the same earth.

————————

Every dragon gives birth to a St. George who slays it.

————————

Trees are poems that the earth writes upon the sky. We fell them down and turn them into paper that we may record our emptiness.

————————

Should you care to write (and only the saints know why you should) you must needs have knowledge and art and magic—the knowledge of the music of words, the art of being artless, and the magic of loving your readers.

————————

They dip their pens in our hearts and think they are inspired.

————————

Should a tree write its autobiography it would not be unlike the history of a race.

————————

If I were to choose between the power of writing a poem and the ecstasy of a poem unwritten, I would choose the ecstasy. It is better poetry.

————————

But you and all my neighbours agree that I always choose badly.

————————

Poetry is not an opinion expressed. It is a song that rises from a bleeding wound or a smiling mouth.

————————

Words are timeless. You should utter them or write them with a knowledge of their timelessness.

————————

A poet is a dethroned king sitting among the ashes of his palace trying to fashion an image out of the ashes.

————————

Poetry is a deal of joy and pain and wonder, with a dash of the dictionary.

————————

In vain shall a poet seek the mother of the songs of his heart.

————————

Once I said to a poet, "We shall not know your worth until you die." And he answered, saying, "Yes, death is always the revealer. And if indeed you would know my worth, it is that I have more in my heart than upon my tongue, and more in my desire than in my hand."

———

If you sing of beauty, though alone in the heart of the desert, you will have an audience.

———

Poetry is wisdom that enchants the heart. Wisdom is poetry that sings in the mind.

If we could enchant man's heart and at the same time sing in his mind, then in truth he would live in the shadow of God.

———

Inspiration will always sing; inspiration will never explain.

———

We often sing lullabies to our children that we ourselves may sleep.

———

All our words are but crumbs that fall down from the feast of the mind.

———

Thinking is always the stumbling stone to poetry.

———

A great singer is he who sings our silences.

———

How can you sing if your mouth be filled with food?
How shall your hand be raised in blessing if it is filled with gold?

———

They say the nightingale pierces his bosom with a thorn when he sings a love song. So do we all. How else should we sing?

———

Genius is but a robin's song at the beginning of a slow spring.

———

Even the most winged spirit cannot escape physical necessity.

———

A madman is not less a musician than you or myself; only the instrument on which he plays is a little out of tune.

———

The song that lies silent in the heart of a mother sings upon the lips of her child.

———

No longing remains unfulfilled.

———

I have never agreed with my other self wholly. The truth of the matter seems to lie between us.

Your other self is always sorry for you. But your other self grows on sorrow; so all is well.

There is no struggle of soul and body save in the minds of those whose souls are asleep and whose bodies are out of tune.

When you reach the heart of life you shall find beauty in all things, even in the eyes that are blind to beauty.

We live only to discover beauty. All else is a form of waiting.

Sow a seed and the earth will yield you a flower. Dream your dream to the sky and it will bring you your beloved.

The devil died the very day you were born.
Now you do not have to go through hell to meet an angel.

Many a woman borrows a man's heart; very few could possess it.

If you would possess you must not claim. When a man's hand touches the hand of a woman they both touch the heart of eternity.

Love is the veil between lover and lover.

Every man loves two women; the one is the creation of his imagination, and the other is not yet born.

Men who do not forgive women their little faults will never enjoy their great virtues.

Love that does not renew itself every day becomes a habit and in turn a slavery.

Lovers embrace that which is between them rather than each other.

Love and doubt have never been on speaking terms.

Love is a word of light, written by a hand of light, upon a page of light.

Friendship is always a sweet responsibility, never an opportunity.

Friendship is always a sweet responsibility, never an opportunity.

If you do not understand your friend under all conditions you will never understand him.

Your most radiant garment is of the other person's weaving;
Your most savoury meal is that which you eat at the other person's table;
Your most comfortable bed is in the other person's house.
Now tell me, how can you separate yourself from the other person?

Your mind and my heart will never agree until your mind ceases to live in numbers and my heart in the mist.

We shall never understand one another until we reduce the language to seven words.

How shall my heart be unsealed unless it be broken?

Only great sorrow or great joy can reveal your truth.
If you would be revealed you must either dance naked in the sun, or carry your cross.

Should Nature heed what we say of contentment no river would seek the sea, and no winter would turn to spring. Should she heed all we say of thrift, how many of us would be breathing this air?

You see but your shadow when you turn your back to the sun.

You are free before the sun of the day, and free before the stars of the night;
And you are free when there is no sun and no moon and no star.
You are even free when you close your eyes upon all there Is.
But you are a slave to him whom you love because you love him.
And a slave to him who loves you because he loves you.

We are all beggars at the gate of the temple, and each one of us receives his share of the bounty of the King when he enters the temple, and when he goes out.
But we are all jealous of one another, which is another way of

belittling the King,

———————

You cannot consume beyond your appetite.
The other half of the loaf belongs to the other person, and there should remain a little bread for the chance guest.

———————

If it were not for guests, all houses would be graves.

———————

Said a gracious wolf to a simple sheep, "Will you not honour our house with a visit?"
And the sheep answered: "We would have been honoured to visit your house if it were not in your stomach."

———————

I stopped my guest on the threshold and said, "Nay, wipe not your feet as you enter, but as you go out."

———————

Generosity is not in giving me that which I need more than you do, but it is in giving me that which you need more than I do.

———————

You are indeed charitable when you give, and while giving turn your face away so that you may not see the shyness of the receiver.

———————

The difference between the richest man and the poorest is but a day of hunger and an hour of thirst.

———————

We often borrow from our to-morrows to pay our debts to our yesterdays.

———————

I too am visited by angels and devils, but I get rid of them.
When it is an angel I pray an old prayer, and he is bored;
"When it is a devil I commit an old sin, and he passes me by.

———————

After all, this not a bad prison; but I do not like this wall between my cell and the next prisoner's cell;
Yet I assure you that I do not wish to reproach the warder nor the Builder of the prison.

———————

Those who give you a serpent when you ask for a fish may have nothing but serpents to give. It is then generosity on their part.

———————

Trickery succeeds sometimes, but it always commits suicide.

———————

You are truly a forgiver when you forgive murderers who never

spill blood, thieves who never steal, and liars who utter no falsehood,

————

He who can put his finger upon that which divides good from evil
is he who can touch the very hem of the garment of God.

————

If your heart is a volcano how shall you expect flowers to bloom
in your hands?

————

A strange form of self-indulgence! There are times when I would
be wronged and cheated, that I may laugh at the expense of those
who think I do not know I am being wronged and cheated.

————

What shall I say of him who is the pursuer playing the part of
the pursued?

————

Let him who wipes his soiled hands with your garment take your
garment. He may need it again; surely you would not.

————

It is a pity that money-changers cannot be good gardeners.

————

Please do not whitewash your inherent faults with your acquired
virtues. I would have the faults; they are like mine own.

————

How often have I attributed to myself crimes I have never committed, so that the other person may feel comfortable in my pres-
ence.

————

Even the masks of life are masks of deeper mystery.

————

You may judge others only according to your knowledge of yourself.
Tell me now, who among us is guilty and who is unguilty?

————

The truly just is he who feels half guilty of your misdeeds.

————

Only an idiot and a genius break man-made laws; and they are
the nearest to the heart of God.

————

It is only when you are pursued that you become swift.

————

I have no enemies, O God, but if I am to have an enemy,
Let his strength be equal to mine,

That truth alone may be the victor.

———————

You will be quite friendly with your enemy when you both die.

———————

Perhaps a man may commit suicide in self-defense.

———————

Long ago there lived a Man who was crucified for being too loving and too lovable.

And, strange to relate, I met Him thrice yesterday.

The first time He was asking a policeman not to take a prostitute to prison; the second time He was drinking wine with an outcast; and the third time He was having a fist-fight with a promoter inside a church.

———————

If all they say of good and evil were true, then my life is but one long crime.

———————

Pity is but half justice.

———————

The only one who has been unjust to me is the one to whose brother I have been unjust.

———————

"When you see a man led to prison, say in your heart, "Mayhap he is escaping from a narrower prison."

And when you see a man drunken, say in your heart, "Mayhap he sought escape from something still more unbeautiful."

———————

Oftentimes I have hated in self-defense; but if I were stronger I would not have used such a weapon.

———————

How stupid is he who would patch the hatred in his eyes with the smile of his lips.

———————

Only those beneath me can envy or hate me.

I have never been envied or hated; I am above no one.

Only those above me can praise or belittle me.

I have never been praised nor belittled; I am below no one.

———————

Your saying to me, "I do not understand you," is praise beyond my worth, and an insult you do not deserve.

———————

How mean am I when life gives me gold and I give you silver, and yet I deem myself generous.

When you reach the heart of life you will find yourself not higher than the felon, and not lower than the prophet.

Strange that you should pity the slow-footed and not the slow-minded,
And the blind-eyed rather than the blind-hearted.

It is wiser for the lame not to break his crutches upon the head of his enemy.

How blind is he who gives you out of his pocket that he may take out of your heart.

Life is a procession. The slow of foot finds it too swift and he steps out;
And the swift of foot finds it too slow and he too steps out.

If there is such a thing as sin, some of us commit it backward following our forefathers' footsteps;
And some of us commit it forward by overruling our children.

The truly good is he who is one with all those who are deemed bad.

We are all prisoners, but some of us are in cells with windows and some without.

Strange that we all defend our wrongs with more vigour than we do our rights.

Should we all confess our sins to one another we would all laugh at one another for our lack of originality.

Should we all reveal our virtues we would also laugh for the same cause.

An individual is above man-made laws until he commits a crime against man-made conventions;
After that he is neither above anyone nor lower than anyone.

Government is an agreement between you and myself. You and myself are often wrong.

Crime is either another name of need or an aspect of a disease.

———————

Is there a greater fault than being conscious of the other person's faults?

———————

If the other person laughs at you, you can pity him; but if you laugh at him you may never forgive yourself.

If the other person injures you, you may forget the injury; but if you injure him you will always remember.

In truth the other person is your most sensitive self given another body.

———————

How heedless you are when you would have men fly with your wings and you cannot even give them a feather.

———————

Once a man sat at my board and ate my bread and drank my wine and went away laughing at me.

Then he came again for bread and wine, and I spurned him;

And the angels laughed at me.

———————

Hate is a dead thing. Who of you would be a tomb?

———————

It is the honour of the murdered that he is not the murderer.

———————

The tribune of humanity is in its silent heart, never its talkative mind.

———————

They deem me mad because I will not sell my days for gold;

And I deem them mad because they think my days have a price.

———————

They spread before us their richest of gold and silver, of ivory and ebony, and we spread before them our hearts and our spirits;

And yet they deem themselves the hosts and us the guests.

———————

I would be the least among men with dreams and the desire to fulfill them, rather than the greatest with no dreams and no desires.

———————

The most pitiful among men is he who turns his dreams into silver and gold.

———————

We are all climbing toward the summit of our hearts' desire. Should the other climber steal your sack and your purse and wax fat on the one and heavy on the other, you should pity him;

The climbing will be harder for his flesh, and the burden will make his way longer.

And should you in your leanness see his flesh puffing upward, help him a step; it will add to your swiftness.

———

You cannot judge any man beyond your knowledge of him, and how small is your knowledge.

———

I would not listen to a conqueror preaching to the conquered.

———

The truly free man is he who bears the load of the bond slave patiently.

———

A thousand years ago my neighbour said to me "I hate life, for it is naught but a thing of pain."

And yesterday I passed by a cemetery and saw life dancing upon his grave.

———

Strife in nature is but disorder longing for order.

———

Yet it sends our living roots deeper into the living heart of the living earth.

———

Once I of the sea to a brook, and the brook thought me but an imaginative exaggerator;

And once I spoke of a brook to the sea, the sea thought me but a depreciative defamer.

———

How narrow is the vision that exalts the busyness of the ant above the singing of the grasshopper.

———

The highest virtue here may be the least in another world.

———

The deep and the high go to the depth or to the height in a straight line; only the spacious can move in circles.

———

If it were not for our conception of weights and measures we would stand in awe of the firefly as we do before the sun.

———

A scientist without imagination is a butcher with dull knives and outworn scales.

But what would you, since we are not all vegetarians?

___

When you sing, the hungry hears you with his stomach.

___

Death is not nearer to the aged than to the new-born; neither is life.

___

If indeed you must be candid, be candid beautifully; otherwise keep silent, for there is a man in our neighbourhood who is dying.

___

Mayhap a funeral among men is a wedding feast among the angels.

___

A forgotten reality may die and leave in its will seven actualities facts to be spent in its funeral and the building of a tomb.

___

In truth we talk only to ourselves, but sometimes we talk loud enough that others may hear us.

___

The obvious is that which is never seen until someone expresses it simply.

___

If the Milky Way were not within me, how should I have seen it or known it?

___

Unless I am a physician among physicians they would not believe that I am an astronomer.

___

Perhaps the sea's definition of a shell is the pearl.
Perhaps time's definition of coal is the diamond.

___

Fame is the shadow of passion standing in the light.

___

A root is a flower that disdains fame.

___

There is neither religion nor science beyond beauty.

___

Every great man I have known had something small in his make-up; and it was that small something which prevented inactivity or madness or suicide.

___

The truly great man is he who would master no one, and who would be mastered by none.

___

I would not believe that man is mediocre, simply because he kills the criminals the prophets.

_____

Tolerance is love sick with the sickness of haughtiness.

_____

Worms will turn; but is it not strange that even elephants will yield?

_____

A disagreement may be the shortest cut between two minds.

_____

I am the flame and I am the dry brush, and one part of me consumes the other part.

_____

We are all seeking the summit of the holy mountain; but not our road be shorter if we consider the past a chart and not a guide?

_____

Wisdom ceases to be wisdom when it becomes too proud to weep, too grave to laugh, too self-ful to see other than itself.

_____

Had I filled myself with all that you know, what room should I have for all that you do not know?

_____

I have learned silence from the talkative, toleration from the intolerant, and kindness from the unkind; yet, strange, I am ungrateful to these teachers.

_____

A bigot is a stone-deaf orator.

_____

The silence of the envious is too noisy.

_____

When you reach the end of what you should know, you will be at the beginning of what you should sense.

_____

An exaggeration is a truth that has lost its temper.

_____

If you can see only what light reveals hear only what sound announces,
Then In truth you do not see nor do you hear.

_____

A fact is a truth unsexed.

_____

You cannot laugh and be unkind at the same time.

_____

The nearest to my heart are a king without a kingdom and a poor man who does not know how to beg.

A shy failure is nobler than an immodest success.

Dig anywhere in the earth and you will find a treasure, only you must dig with the faith of a peasant.

Said a hunted fox followed by twenty horsemen and a pack of twenty hounds, "Of course they will kill me. But how poor and how stupid they must be. Surely it would not be worthwhile for twenty foxes riding on twenty asses and accompanied by twenty wolves to chase and kill one man."

It is the mind in us that yields to the laws made by us, but never the spirit in us.

A traveller am I and a navigator, and every day I discover a new region within my soul.

A woman protested saying, "Of course it was a righteous war. My son fell in it."

I said to Life, "I would hear Death speak."
And Life raised her voice a little higher said, "You hear him now."

When you have solved ail the mysteries of life you long for death, for it is but another mystery of life.
Birth and death are the two noblest expressions of bravery.

My friend, you and I shall remain strangers unto life,
And unto one another, and each unto himself.
Until the day when you shall speak and I shall listen,
Deeming your voice my own voice;
And when I shall stand before you
Thinking myself standing before a mirror.

They say to me, "Should you know yourself you would know all men."
And I say, "Only when I seek all men shall
I know myself,"

Man is two men; one is awake in darkness, the other is asleep
In light.

A hermit is one who renounces the world of fragments that he may enjoy the world wholly and without interruption.

———

There lies a green field between the scholar and the poet; should the scholar cross it, he becomes a wise man; should the poet cross it, he becomes a prophet,

———

Yestereve I saw philosophers in the marketplace carrying their heads in crying aloud,
"Wisdom! Wisdom for sale!"
Poor philosophers! They sell their heads to feed their hearts.

———

Said a philosopher to a street sweeper, "I pity you. Yours is a hard dirty task."
And the street sweeper said,, "Thank you, sir. But tell me, what is your task?"
And the philosopher answered, saying,
"I study man's mind, his deeds his desires."
Then the street sweeper went on with his sweeping and said with a smile, "I pity you too."

———

He who listens to truth Is not less than, he who utters truth.

———

No man can draw the line between necessities and luxuries. Only the angels can do that, and the angels are wise and wistful.
Perhaps the angels are our better thoughts in space.

———

He is the true prince who finds his throne in the heart of the dervish.

———

Generosity is giving more than you can, and pride is taking less than you need.

———

In truth you owe naught to any man. You all to all men.

———

All those who have lived in the past live with us now. Surely none of us would be an ungracious host

———

He who longs the most lives the longest.

———

They say to me, "A bird In the hand is worth ten In the bush."
But I say, "A bird and a feather in the bush is worth more than ten birds in the hand."

Your seeking after that feather is life with winged feet; nay, it is life Itself.

There are only two elements here, beauty and truth; beauty in the hearts of lovers, and truth in the arms of the tillers of the soil.

Great beauty captures me, but a beauty still greater frees me even from itself.

Beauty shines brighter in the heart of him who longs for it than in the eyes of him who sees it.

I admire the man who reveals his mind to me; I honour him who unveils his dreams.

But why am I shy, and even a little ashamed, before him who serves me?

The gifted were once proud in serving princes.

Now they claim honour in serving paupers.

The angels know too many practical men eat bread with the sweat of the dreamer's brow.

Wit is often a mask. If you could tear it you would either a genius irritated or cleverness juggling.

The understanding attributes to me understanding and the dull dullness. I think they are right.

Only those with secrets in their hearts could divine the secrets in our hearts.

He who would share your pleasure but not your pain shall lose the key to one of the seven gates of Paradise.

Yes there is a Nirvanah; it is in leading your sheep to a green pasture, and in putting your child to sleep, and in writing the last line of your poem.

We choose our joys and our sorrows long before we experience them.

Sadness is but a wall between two gardens.

When either your joy or your sorrow becomes great the world becomes small.

Desire is half of life; indifference is half of death.

The bitterest thing In our to-day's sorrow is the memory of our yesterday's joy.

They say to me, "You must needs choose between the pleasures of this world and the peace of the next world."
And I say to them, "I have chosen both the delights of this world and the peace of the next. For I know in my heart that the Supreme Poet wrote but one poem, it scans perfectly, it rhymes perfectly."

Faith is an oasis in the heart which will never be reached by the caravan of thinking.

When you reach your height you shall desire, but only for desire; and you shall hunger for hunger; and you shall thirst for greater thirst.

If you reveal your secrets to the wind you should not blame the wind for revealing them to the trees.

The flowers of spring are winter's dreams related at the breakfast table of the angels.

Said a skunk to a tuberose, "See how swiftly
I run, while you cannot walk nor even creep." Said the tuberose to the skunk, "Oh, noble swift runner, please run swiftly!"

Turtles can tell more about the roads than hares.

Strange that creatures without backbones have the hardest shells.

The most talkative Is the least intelligent, and there is hardly a difference between an orator and an auctioneer.

Be grateful that you do not have to live down the renown of a father nor the wealth of an uncle.
But above all be grateful that no one will have to live down either

your renown or your wealth.

———

Only when a juggler misses catching his ball does he appeal to me.

———

The envious praises me unknowingly.

———

Long were you a dream in your mother's sleep, and then she woke to give you birth.

———

The germ of the race is in your mother's longing.

———

My father and mother desired a child and they begot me.
And I wanted a mother and a father and I begot night and the sea.

———

Some of our children are our justifications and some are but our regrets.

———

When night comes and you too are dark, lie down and be dark with a will.
And when morning comes and you are still dark, stand up and say to the day with a will,
"I am still dark"
It is stupid to play a role with the night and the day.
They would both laugh at you.

———

The mountain veiled in mist is not a hill; an oak tree in the rain is not a weeping willow.

———

Behold, here is a paradox: the deep and high are nearer to one another than the mid-lever to either.

———

When I stood a clear mirror before you, you gazed into me and saw your image.
Then you said, "I love you."
But in truth you loved yourself in me.

———

When you enjoy loving your neighbour it ceases to be a virtue.

———

Love which is not always springing is always dying.

———

You cannot have youth and the knowledge of it at the same time;

For youth is too busy living to know, and knowledge is too busy seeking itself to live.

You may sit at your window watching the passers-by. And watching you may see a nun walking toward your right hand, and a prostitute toward your left hand.

And you may say in your innocence, "How noble is the one and how ignoble is the other."

And should you close your eyes and listen awhile you would hear a voice whispering in the ether, "One seeks me in prayer, and the other in pain. And in the spirit of each there is a bower for my spirit."

Once every hundred years Jesus of Nazareth meets Jesus of the Christian in a garden among the hills of Lebanon. And they talk long; and each time Jesus of Nazareth goes away saying to Jesus of the Christian, "My friend, I fear we shall never, never agree."

May God feed the over-abundant!

A great man has two hearts: one bleeds the other forbears.

Should one tell a lie which does not hurt you nor anyone else, why not say in your heart that the house of his facts is too small for his fancies, and he had to leave it for larger space?

Behind every closed door is a mystery sealed with seven seals.

Waiting is the hoofs of time.

What if trouble should be a new window in the Eastern wall of your house?

You may forget the one with whom you have laughed, but never the one with whom you have wept.

There be something strangely sacred in salt.
It is in our tears and in the sea.

Our God In His gracious thirst will drink us all, the dewdrop and the tear.

You are but a fragment of your giant self, a mouth that bread, and a blind hand that holds the cup for a thirsty mouth.

———————

If you would rise but a cubit above race and country and self you would indeed become godlike.

———————

If I were you I would not find fault with the sea at low tide.
It is a good ship and our Captain is able; it
Is only your stomach that is in disorder.

———————

What we long for and cannot attain is dearer than what we have already attained.

———————

Should you sit upon a cloud you would not see the boundary line between one country another, nor the boundary stone between a farm and a farm.
It is a pity you cannot sit upon a cloud.

———————

Seven centuries ago seven white doves rose from a deep valley flying to the snow-white summit of the mountain. One of the seven who watched the flight said, "I see a black spot on the wing of the seventh dove."
To-day the people in that valley tell of seven black doves that flew to the summit of the snowy mountain.

———————

In the autumn I gathered all my sorrows and buried them in my garden.
And when April returned and spring came to wed the earth, there grew in my garden beautiful flowers unlike all other flowers.
And my neighbours came to behold them, and they all said to me, ""When autumn comes again, at seeding time, will you not give us of the seeds of these flowers that we may have them in our gardens?"

———————

It is indeed misery if I stretch an empty hand to men to receive nothing; but it is hopeless if I stretch a full hand and find none to receive.

———————

I long for eternity because there I shall meet my unwritten poems and my unplanted pictures

———————

Art is a step from nature toward the infinite.

———————

A work of art is a mist carved into an image.

Even the hands that make crowns of thorns are better than idle hands.

Our most sacred tears never seek our eyes.

Every man is the descendant of every king and every slave ever lived.

If the great-grandfather of Jesus had known what was hidden within him, would he not have stood in awe of himself?

Was the love of Judas' mother for her son less than the love of Mary for Jesus?

You may have heard of the Blessed Mountain
It is the highest mountain in our world.
Should you reach the summit you would have only one desire, and that to descend and be with those who dwell in the deepest valley.
That is why it is called the Blessed Mountain.

Every thought I have imprisoned in expression I must free by my deeds.

CPSIA information can be obtained at www.ICGtesting.com
Printed in the USA
LVOW100006110912

298266LV00013B/154/P